THE NEXT GENERATION

SMALL GROUP LEADERS'
HANDBOOK

WRITTEN BY A SMALL GROUP CONSISTING OF

JIMMY LONG (COORDINATOR),
ANN BEYERLEIN, SARA KEIPER, PATTY PELL,
NINA THIEL & DOUG WHALLON

IVP Connect

An imprint of InterVarsity Press
Downers Grove, Illinois

InterVarsity Press
P.O. Box 1400, Downers Grove, IL 60515-1426
World Wide Web: www.ivpress.com
E-mail: email@ivpress.com

InterVarsity Press® is the book-publishing division of InterVarsity Christian Fellowship/USA®, a student movement active on campus at hundreds of universities, colleges and schools of nursing in the United States of America, and a member movement of the International Fellowship of Evangelical Students. For information about local and regional activities, write Public Relations Dept., InterVarsity Christian Fellowship/USA, 6400 Schroeder Rd., P.O. Box 7895, Madison, WI 53707-7895, or visit the IVCF website at <www.intervarsity.org>.

All Scripture quotations, unless otherwise indicated, are taken from the Holy Bible, New International Version®. NIV®. Copyright ©1973, 1978, 1984 by International Bible Society. Used by permission of Zondervan Publishing House. All rights reserved.

Cartoons on pages 182 and 196 used by permission of Rob Suggs.

Artwork in chapter thirteen is by Kathy Alred Lin and is used by permission.

Design: Cindy Kiple
Images: bean bag with glasses: Alex Wilson/Digital Vision
        blue bean bag: Paul Taylor/Getty Images
        red bean bag: Davies and Starr/Getty Images

ISBN 978-0-8308-1139-7

Printed in the United States of America ∞

Library of Congress Cataloging-in-Publication Data

Small group leaders' handbook: the next generation/written by a
   small group consisting of Jimmy Long . . . [et al.].
      p. cm.
   Includes bibliographical references.
      ISBN 0-8308-1139-7 (pbk.: alk. paper)
      1. Church group work with young adults.   I. Long, Jimmy.
   BV4446.S59   1995
   259'.23—dc20   95-43636
                                                                                CIP

P	28	27	26	25	24	23	22	21	20	19	18	17	16	15	14	13	12
Y	22	21	20	19	18	17	16	15	14	13	12	11	10	09	08	07	

Introduction ——————————————— 7

PART 1/EXPLORING OUR MISSION ———————— 11

1/A New Generation of Small Groups ————— 13

2/A Biblical Voyage Through Small Groups ———— 23

PART 2/SETTING OUR COURSE ——————— 37

3/Building Relationships: Community —————— 39

4/Developing Disciples: Nurture ——————— 53

5/Adoring God: Worship & Prayer ————— 69

6/Becoming Witnesses: Outreach ————— 85

PART 3/NAVIGATING GROUP LIFE ————— 101

7/Guiding Through Phases ——————— 103

8/Cultivating Group Ownership ————— 119

9/Encouraging Good Communication ———— 131

10/Redeeming Conflict ——————— 145

PART 4/SERVING AT THE HELM ————— 159

11/The Growing Leader ——————— 161

12/The Influencing Leader ——————— 177

13/The Organizing Leader ——————— 189

Introduction

To boldly go where no one has gone before. This was the task of the InterVarsity Christian Fellowship staff team (Steve Barker, Judy Johnson, Jimmy Long, Rob Malone and Ron Nicholas) who created the *Small Group Leaders' Handbook,* published in 1982. Used by a variety of groups, including prison ministries and Officers Christian Fellowship, that groundbreaking book was of great service to both the campus and the church.

To reach the next generation. That is the mission given to the authors of this completely rewritten handbook.

The authors embarking on this new adventure in small group life were led by the group coordinator, Jimmy Long, regional director for the Blue Ridge Region and a small group ministry pioneer in IVCF. With his doctor of ministry studies in the areas of postmodernism and Generation X, Jimmy served well as a coordinator with a lion's courage as we faced group conflict and a lamb's quiet spirit as he listened to us all.

Ann Beyerlein, a staffworker at Northwestern University in Evanston, Illinois, brought to the group her understanding of ministry in a multi-ethnic context and her desire to help students build healthy friendships. Ann's organizational skills helped us immensely in putting the chapters together—and she shared her alarm clock with us when we needed it.

Sara Keiper's ministry from coast to coast (San Francisco to Philadelphia) has included work with nursing students and other IVCF students. Currently on staff at the University of Pennsylvania, Sara dazzled us with her ability to hang spoons on her face. More importantly, she challenged us with her vulnerability and her history of caring for others through the darkest of days.

Patty "Side Bar" Pell inspired us with her passion for understanding and applying Scripture. Always ready to preach the Word, Patty works with students at the University of Northern Colorado. The youngest of the group and an Xer, Patty's joyful personality kept us feeling lively through long days of work.

Nina (!) Thiel brought to the book her experience with commuter and residential students from diverse backgrounds and her passion for outreach. Her gentle spirit and deep convictions inspired us, and we found her friendly writing style so appealing that we assigned her an extra chapter! Nina is currently a field staffworker at the University of Nevada, Las Vegas, in IVCF's Southern California region.

Doug Whallon, New England Regional Director, graciously put aside some serious back pain to meet with us, even sacrificing himself to the point of offering to play basketball. With chapters rich in thoughtful wording and insight, Doug brought depth to our discussions, helping us keep kingdom issues in mind. And when dinnertime came around, he was always ready to guide us to the finer restaurants in Massachusetts.

This book is a collaborative effort. Early in the process of deciding to do this book, Jimmy Long and Doug Whallon met with Richard Peace. We appreciate the encouragement he gave us to do the book and the guidance we received from him on the way. We also appreciate the insights gained at the 1994 Small Group Conference at Eastern College. And we are grateful to Greg Jao for his careful analysis and suggestions for revision—lengthy enough to rival the chapters themselves.

The original *Small Group Leaders' Handbook* included a resource section. We expanded that much-used feature with new ideas from InterVarsity staff and students from across the country. We particularly want to thank the Downstate Illinois team, who submitted the most ideas of any area and won a pizza party. Runners-up included Central/South New

Jersey and Western Washington. You'll find these invaluable resources for community, worship and prayer, nurture and outreach in a companion volume, *Small Group Idea Book*. We suggest that you read and use these two books together.

On each chapter you'll find the name of the author who drafted the material, but we all discussed and contributed to each chapter. The basic small group philosophy in this book is one we agreed on together. We hope that your small group will benefit from our small group experience in writing this book.

Your mission: To boldly go and lead a small group. Will you accept it?

Cindy Bunch, Editor
1995

PART 1
EXPLORING OUR MISSION

1/A New Generation of
  Small Groups

2/A Biblical Voyage
  Through Small Groups

Popular culture shows the influence of growing numbers of Christian broadcast majors.

"...IT'S ALSO PART OF OUR CONTINUING MISSION TO SEEK OUT THE UNSAVED, TO DISCOVER UNCHURCHED WORLDS, TO BOLDLY GO WHERE NO MISSIONARY HAS GONE BEFORE!"

HALL

1/A NEW GENERATION OF SMALL GROUPS
■ Jimmy Long

Captain's Log, Stardate 486650.1

I keep pondering over what Captain Kirk told me earlier today.
"Picard, don't let them promote you, don't let them transfer you,
don't let anything take you off the bridge of that ship. Because
while you're there (and in command of the *Enterprise*), you can
make a difference." I want to make a difference! I, oh, so want to
make a difference. *(Star Trek: Generations)*

Author's Log, Earthdate Fall 1995

It is my hope that you, like Picard, want to make a difference. A
small group leader has a role of strategic importance similar to
that of serving the U.S.S. *Enterprise*. You, however, have the opportunity
to influence people for eternity. As serving at the helm of the *Enterprise*
is both a challenging responsibility and a privilege, so is leading a small
group. Having six to twelve people under your leadership can feel daunt-
ing at times. However, seeing those same small group members grow
closer to each other and to God, while at the same time reaching out to
bring new people into the group, will bring you great satisfaction.

For Kirk and Picard a key to successful leadership was maintaining
an overall perspective of their mission. They needed to understand *why*
they were on their mission. They also had to have a grasp of *what* were
the components of their mission and set their course. Furthermore,
through mapping out and navigating a course, they began to understand

how to proceed in their mission. To accomplish their mission they had to grasp *who* they were as leaders and be willing to serve at the helm.

As small group leaders, we also need to keep an overall perspective. Too often we concentrate only on the hows of the next meeting. By covering the whys, whats, hows and whos of small groups, this book will help you keep the larger picture in mind. In the first two chapters we will work on the whys of small groups by exploring our mission. We will set our course in chapters three through six by looking at the whats of small groups. "Navigating group life" will be our theme in chapters seven through ten as we look at the hows of small groups. In chapters eleven through thirteen we will focus on the whos of small groups as we concentrate on our role of "serving at the helm."

Setting the Stage

Small groups have always been a part of InterVarsity's existence in the United States. In the 1940s the qualifications to become an InterVarsity campus group at such places as the University of Michigan and the University of Illinois were a daily prayer meeting and weekly Bible studies. The importance of small groups continued after World War II at places like Texas A & M, which had 600 students involved in over forty InterVarsity Bible studies. In the late 1960s small groups made a resurgence following the publication of InterVarsity's November 1968 edition of *HIS* magazine, devoted entirely to small groups. In the early 1980s many InterVarsity groups experienced rapid growth and students desired to be more anonymous; large groups began to be more the central focus for many campus groups.

As the 21st century begins, we are experiencing a cultural shift which could be as dramatic as the shift from the Middle Ages to the Renaissance. Although it is sometimes difficult to identify because it is happening slowly over an extended period of time, we need to try to understand the changes and adjust our ministry to meet the needs. Small groups will have a major part in outreach and discipleship on campus as we move into this new cultural era.

Facing change can be intimidating, but the apostle Paul provides an encouraging example. As Paul entered Athens, a new cultural context for the gospel, he pondered how to bring the eternally true gospel to a radically different culture. Paul applied three different strategies as he proclaimed the everlasting gospel of Jesus Christ. Instead of preaching or teaching as he had done before in previous cities, Paul reasoned with the Athenians in the synagogue and marketplace (Acts 17:17). Second, Paul, instead of initially talking about Yahweh, connected with the Athenians through the example of their altar "TO AN UNKNOWN GOD" (v. 23). Finally, instead of referring to the Old Testament prophets, he quoted a Greek poet to help the Athenians to identify with his message (v. 28). As Paul recognized and responded to the changing cultural values between the Jewish and Hellenistic worlds, we need to understand the shift in cultural values within our society.

Who Are We?

At a recent Harvard graduation ceremony, one of the student speakers summarized how many people today are feeling in the midst of this cultural value shift.

> I believe that there is one idea, one sentiment, which we have all acquired at some point in our Harvard careers, and that ladies and gentlemen is in a word, confusion. They tell us that it is heresy to suggest the superiority of some value, fantasy to believe in moral argument, slavery to submit to a judgement sounder than your own. The freedom of our day is the freedom to devote ourselves to any values we please, on the mere condition that we do not believe them to be true.

Confusion is intensified today because there are two primary shifts occurring at the same time. One of these shifts is from Baby Boomers to Generation X and eventually to the Post Xer (Millennial) Generation. At the same time an even larger cultural paradigm shift is occurring from the Enlightenment era (1500-1968) of the Baby Boomers and those before them to postmodernism (1968 on). Generation X is the first "pure" postmodern generation. The contrast in the eras can be characterized as follows:

Enlightenment	Postmodernism
truth	preferences
autonomous self	community
scientific discovery	virtual reality
human progress	human misery

There are a number of specific effects on college students stemming from this transition into postmodernism. We now live in a world with few traditions and little basis for decision-making. Instead of traditions like family values or moral ethical consensus, we only have preferences. The result is a sense that anything goes. Many students today are wandering through the night groping for guidance.

In response, students are developing their own community groups which help them make sense of life. The political Right, gay/lesbian and even certain Christian groups have come together to form their own truths, many times at the exclusion of others. So today, instead of coming together, postmodernism is causing many students to move apart and stay in their own groups (sometimes called *tribal groups*) to develop some security and significance.

Another reason for the development of these groups is the onslaught of the dysfunctional family due at least in part to the sexual rebellion of the Boomers and the breakdown of the two-parent family. These family changes stemmed from the Boomers' desire for independence and self-fulfillment. Fifty percent of today's teenagers are not living with both their original mother and original father. In a recent survey, while 80% of divorced parents professed to being happier after the divorce, only 20% of the children said they were happier after the divorce.

We cope with the disappointment and pain of childhood in a number of ways. For many, friends take the place of family. Friends matter enormously. A mutual-protection circle of friends provides a guard against the

"I don't care if it is 2025 . . . this church was built on its outreach to baby boomers and it's going to stay that way!"

cruel adolescent world. We feel safe among friends. This need for close friends continues in college.

The Small Group Strategy

As we look at the deep needs for security and significance being met through friendships and community, we need to make sure we adjust our ministry to meet these real needs of students. Small group ministry is a key to meeting these needs. In a recent *Christianity Today* article, Robert Wuthnow, a leading sociologist, explains: "We no longer live in the same neighborhoods all our lives or retain close ties with our kin. The small group movement has arisen out of the breakdown of these traditional support structures and from our continuing desire for community. We want others with whom we can share our journey."

If we are going to faithfully minister to our student generation in the coming years, InterVarsity campus groups can no longer be a fellowship that contains small groups, but a fellowship of small groups. Small groups need to be at the heart of accomplishing InterVarsity's vision, which is to

BUILD COLLEGIATE FELLOWSHIPS

DEVELOP DISCIPLES who embody biblical values and

ENGAGE THE CAMPUS in all its ethnic diversity with the gospel of Jesus Christ.

Building Fellowships

Consider two questions: (1) What are students in your chapter referring to when they say they are going to InterVarsity this week? (2) Are more students in your chapter involved in small groups or the large group meeting?

If you answered "large group" to both of these questions, you might need to rethink your building strategy if you want small groups to be the foundation for your chapter. Students today are desperately seeking a community in which to belong. It is critical for us to provide students the opportunity to be a part of a caring Christian community during those first few days on campus. InterVarsity small groups of six to twelve students are the ideal environment for this Christian community to take shape.

One small group building strategy can been seen in Liz's group in Randall Dorm. Liz and all the other small group leaders in her chapter attended the New Student Picnic which was held a few days before classes even began in the fall. At the picnic all the new students were divided into their dorm units or geographical sections (if they lived off campus) to meet with their potential small group leader. (In some schools this dividing into small groups occurs at the first large group meeting.)

Liz sat down with the six new students from Randall to help them get to know each other and tell them a little bit about the small group in Randall. While visiting each of the new students the next day, Liz invited each of them to go out to eat with the small group that night. Before classes began these new students were involved in a small group.

During the rest of the semester, these new students and the returning students met weekly for their small group in Randall. More than that, they became friends and included each other in all types of outings—meals, movies, ball games, studying and even doing their laundry together.

Liz's small group began with nine students. Because everyone loved the group, they began inviting other friends in Randall to join. By the end of the first semester the group had grown to eighteen, so at the beginning of the second semester they divided into two groups.

When these students thought of InterVarsity, they thought of their small group even though they went to large group meetings together. Although they might miss a large group meeting now and then, they never missed small group because their small group became their friendship group. They connected first with a small community and not with a large gathering. Students today have a deep need for a small community in which they can be known.

Developing Disciples

Students also need a community to help them develop into maturing disciples of Jesus Christ. Students entering college often have very little biblical foundation. Many become Christians while they are in college. They are attracted to Christianity partly because of the community that they experience in small groups. However, we want to make sure that students are converted not just to the Christian community, but to the King of the community—Jesus Christ. To accomplish this goal small group leaders need to help their small group members be disciples of Jesus Christ.

Does developing group members into disciples feel like an overwhelming task? Let me ease your anxiety by telling you how Jonathan helped his members grow.

Jonathan had only been a Christian a few years himself, and his time was limited because he had a part-time job. However, he loved God and his small group members. Jonathan made four commitments to the development of the members of his group. First, he recognized that the primary way Christians develop is through the study of the Bible, so he committed himself to faithfully preparing for the Bible study portion of the small group each week. Next, although Jonathan knew he could not disciple everyone in his group, he decided to disciple two students weekly, and as time permitted he visited other members, who were scattered all over the community.

Jonathan also committed himself to attending large group and any other training event or conference InterVarsity sponsored. Jonathan realized that because he went to a commuter school his small group did not have as many natural opportunities to build friendships as students involved in a residential chapter do. So to all these IVCF events he tried to bring as many of his small group members as he could. At Spring Conference that year Jonathan arrived with all fourteen members of his small group. Finally, Jonathan worked hard to make sure each member of his group was regularly attending church.

Jonathan was faithful in his commitment to the development of his small group members, using the resources available to him. By the end of the year, his small group members were not mature, but they were maturing. Eight out of the fourteen students in his small group were small group leaders the next year.

Engaging the Campus

I would characterize students today as relative cynics. Students of this generation feel abandoned by their dysfunctional families, by a faltering economic system and by a power-hungry political system. All of these conditions have caused many students not to trust anyone. Additionally, as a result of postmodernism, truth has become only preferences. What truth the postmodern student usually has comes about through seeing that truth practiced in a community. Students need to see truth applied, not just proclaimed.

In this climate small groups become the ideal place for evangelism. It is primarily through individual friendships that trust can be established and primarily through observing a small group community that truth will be experienced. Large group events supplement individual and community evangelism.

Jack's small group in Taylor Dorm was not a group that anyone would have expected to hold up as a model small group, but over time they embodied these principles of outreach. The group was composed of seven students—none of whom would be considered particularly bright or socially adept—who grew to love each other and felt a deep compassion for their fellow students in their dorm. Each committed to reaching out in friendship to at least one person in their dorm who was not a Christian.

At first glance some of their choices did not seem likely to be people who would become Christians. For instance, David picked Mike, who was one of the top scholars in his class. David was close to flunking out of school. Two other members in the group, Mary and Andy, picked Eddie, whom everyone, except probably Mary and Andy, knew as the dorm drug dealer. However, over a period of time, Mike came to trust David. Although David could answer very few of Mike's questions, David was the first person who Mike felt ever cared for him. For Eddie, Mary and Andy were the first people in a long time who had cared for him because of who he was and not because he could sell them drugs.

As these friendships were developing, the small group slowly became more and more of a community. One of the members of the small group, Annie, had been ostracized by her Jewish family after she became a Christian. She developed a new appreciation for some of the Jewish festivals from a Christian perspective. Annie helped the other members experience these traditions. After they had invited both Mike and Eddie to some social outings of the group, they began to invite both of them to some of their small group meetings, especially the Jewish festivals.

During the year both Mike and Eddie became Christians. Later Mike was asked what made the difference. He said it certainly was not the intellectual discussions. David did not win one of those debates, but he won Mike's trust. He consistently cared for Mike as a person. Mike began to see that David's caring was the incarnation of Christ's caring for him. Mike also said that he saw within the small group the truth of Christ being lived out in community as he observed people in the small group loving each other and beginning to love him. For Mike the small group was the gospel in action.

Each of the leaders we looked at—Liz, Jonathan and Jack—made a difference. Each of them had different gifts and unique groups. However, God worked in them and through them to develop a small group that changed lives. God wants to work in you and through you to make a difference with your small group.

Understanding the Chapter
Study

1. Read Acts 17:16-34. Trace Paul's strategy in Athens.

2. Compare this strategy with Paul's strategy in more Jewish settings like Pisidian Antioch (Acts 13:13-52).

Reflect

1. What characteristics would you use to describe your student generation?

2. How might these characteristics shape your strategy for ministering to your fellow students?

3. Last year what role did your small group have in accomplishing the vision of building a fellowship, developing disciples and engaging the campus with the gospel?

4. What role do you want this coming year's small group to have in building, developing and engaging the campus?

Apply

1. List ways you would like to make a difference in your small group.

2. Commit yourself to praying daily for members of your small group.

2/A BiBLICaL VOYaGE THrouGH SmaLL GrouPS
■ Jimmy Long

It was a simple question. I only asked it to pass the time before the beginning of a large group meeting. Little did I imagine what the response would bring.

"Are you going home for Christmas?" was the question I innocently asked Joan that December evening. Before I had finished asking the question, Joan burst into tears.

I thought to myself, *What in the world have I done?*

As Joan slowly gathered herself, she told me how she did not really have a home to go back to. Her parents got a divorce when she was ten years old. Now ten years later both her parents had each been married twice more. Joan realized that cold December that she was not sure where—or if—her home was. She did not understand why her past was so confusing.

Too many people, especially students like Joan, have little understanding of or sense of belonging to the past or present. The lyrics of the song

"Homesickness" by Soul Asylum capture this deep longing for origins and a home where we belong.

I want to live with you in the 5th dimension in a dream I've never had

But because I just can't live like this in a world like this, I just want to kiss goodbye

We're not of this world and there is a place for us stuck inside this fleeting moment

Tucked away where no one owns it wrapped up in haste and by mistake thrown away

I am so homesick but oh that's not so bad because I am homesick for the home I've never had

Ultimately, our search for a place to belong will only be satisfied when we find our eternal family. And for many of us our best experience of belonging is being part of the Christian community in small groups—an idea that began at creation.

Created for Community

After Adam was created, God declared, "It is not good for the man to be alone" (Genesis 2:18). Have you ever wondered if God had made a mistake in creation? When he created Adam did he forget to create something in Adam that would make him feel secure and not alone? The answer is an emphatic *no*.

From the very beginning of time God had planned to create all humans to need both God and other humans. He created all of humankind to live in community, a small group community. We see this small group community in creation consisting of God, Adam and Eve. The relationship among the three of them was a prototype of how God wanted to relate to his people and how he wanted them to relate to each other.

The relationship between Adam and Eve lays the foundation for relationships between any others in community. They had no barriers to God or between themselves. Adam could say, "This is now bone of my bones and flesh of my flesh" (Genesis 2:23). The author of Genesis could state, "The man and his wife were both naked, and they felt no shame" (v. 25).

In the beginning Adam and Eve lived in perfect harmony. They felt at home with each other and with God. There was no fear or alienation. Between themselves and with God they lived contented within a small group community.

Rebelling from Community

Eventually, Adam and Eve became discontented. Instead of being willing to be in communion with God and proper community with each other, they sought independence. The result of their sin and rebellion was alienation from God and each other. They now felt shame around each other and thus tried to create barriers between themselves.

Then the eyes of both of them were opened, and they realized they were naked; so they sewed fig leaves together and made coverings for themselves.

They were ashamed and afraid of God, so they tried to hide:

Then the man and his wife heard the sound of the LORD God as he was walking in the garden in the cool of the day, and they hid from the LORD God among the trees of the garden. But the LORD God called to the man, "Where are you?"

He answered, "I heard you in the garden and I was afraid because I was naked; so I hid." (Genesis 3:7-10)

The small group community was shattered. Instead of contentment there was contention. Instead of harmony there was hatred. Instead of sharedness there was shame. The rest of human history became a struggle between humanity's continued rebellion from a small group community on the one hand and its desperate search for that community on the other hand.

Nowhere is this juxtaposition between the rejection of community and our homesickness for community more evident than in Genesis 11 and 12. In Genesis 11 we see humankind's continued rebellion from community with God in their attempt to build a tower to the heavens: "Come let us build ourselves a city, with a tower that reaches to the heavens, so that we may make a name for ourselves and not be scattered over the face of the whole earth" (v. 4).

God realized this attempt at community without his presence would ultimately be unfulfilling, because God has created us to be in small group community with him as well as with each other. God was also righteously jealous of humanity's attempt to take God's place by building a tower to the heavens. As a result, God prevented the building of the Tower of Babel by confusing the languages and scattering the people over the whole earth.

Through the rest of the Old Testament, we continue to see humanity's futile attempts to find community. These attempts continue to fail because they ultimately lead to further rebellion from God and alienation from each other. The end result is despair for all women and men. As we see in Soul Asylum's "Homesickness," the despair still exists today.

Restored to Community

Although humankind rebelled against God in the past and still does so in the present, God did not turn his face from his people. Immediately following the scattering of the people at the Tower of Babel, God gathers together a small group, Abram's family, to begin fulfilling his planned restoration of community.

> The LORD had said to Abram, "Leave your country, your people and your father's household and go to the land I will show you.
>
> "I will make you into a great nation
>   and I will bless you. . . .
> And all peoples on earth
>   will be blessed through you." (Genesis 12:1-3)

Throughout Old Testament history people made sacrifices in partnership with God to try to bring about restored community. Leaders like Abraham, Joseph and Moses gave up their positions of power and comfort to take part in God's planned restoration. They sacrificed even in the midst of rebellion after rebellion by those who wanted to control their own destinies.

These attempts at the restoration of community kept the vision of community before the people. However, by themselves they could not succeed. Something more drastic needed to happen.

Recreated in Community

A totally new creation of humankind in community came when God himself made the sacrifice by sending his Son, Jesus. Jesus' mission was to recreate us in community with God and with each other.

To accomplish his mission, Jesus formed a small group community. "Jesus went up on a mountainside and called to him those he wanted, and they came to him. He appointed twelve—designating them apostles—that they might be with him and that he might send them out to preach" (Mark 3:13-14). Throughout his three years of ministry, Jesus instilled within this small group community a commitment to himself and to each other.

Although not without its problems, this small group of disciples began to recognize Jesus' leadership in their lives. When Jesus asked Peter, "Who do you say I am?" Peter answered, "You are the Christ" (8:29). The disciples had begun to see that they could no longer control their own destiny. They needed to submit to Jesus' authority.

Furthermore, Jesus began to help the disciples recognize that if they were going to be able to form a small group community, they needed to change their attitudes and expectations about their own roles. One day he heard them arguing among themselves, so he said, " 'What were you

arguing about on the road?' But they kept quiet because on the way they had argued about who was the greatest. Sitting down, Jesus called the Twelve and said, 'If anyone wants to be first, he must be the very last, and the servant of all' " (9:33-35).

Time and time again, Jesus demonstrated for the disciples what it meant to serve each other in the small group community. Jesus even washed the disciples' feet, a task performed only by the lowest of servants. He was recreating the kind of small group community that existed among God and Adam and Eve before the Fall.

Jesus sensed immediately before his arrest that his example was almost complete. Soon the disciples would begin their own ministry of reconciliation. So Jesus prayed for the disciples:

I have revealed you to those whom you gave me out of the world. They were yours; you gave them to me and they have obeyed your word. . . .

My prayer is not that you take them out of the world but that you protect them from the evil one. They are not of the world, even as I am not of it. Sanctify them by the truth; your word is truth. As you sent me into the world, I have sent them into the world. (John 17:6, 15-18)

Jesus had done what he needed to to give the disciples a vision of human community. All that was left was to give them a way to re-create the small group community between humanity and God. The only way for him to accomplish that task was to take our deserved punishment and our place on the cross for our rebellion from community with God. Jesus' death on the cross broke down the barrier that existed between men and women and God since that first rebellion soon after creation. The symbol of the restoration of community was the tearing of the temple curtain—which separated the people from God—in the Holy of Holies at the moment of Jesus' death.[1]

Reconciled into Community

The ministry of reconciliation is the ministry of taking people who are alienated from God and each other and building them into a community which deeply cares for each member and allows God to care for them. The house churches of the early church, such as the one meeting in the home of Aquila and Priscilla in Rome (Romans 16:3-5), were the first attempts at forming reconciling small group communities. These small group communities continued in the catacombs of Rome during the persecution of the Christians by the Romans.

Later on in the history of the church these small group communities took on various functions. In the sixth century the Benedictine order was the beginning of the monastic movement. These orders at their best were small group communities which helped preserve the church from the pagan takeovers which took place in Europe during the Middle Ages.

In the twelfth century small group communities like the Waldensians in the Italian Alps formed to try to preserve the truth of the gospel from the increasing corruption within the church. Small group preservation communities continued for the next few centuries until the Reformation.

Following the Reformation, small group communities sprang up once again not as much for preservation purposes but for reconciling purposes. The small group community which probably had the most influence and probably would be recognized as the forerunner of small groups today was the Hernhutt small group community begun by Count Zinzendorf in 1727. The community was divided into small groups called "choirs," which filled the need for intimate sharing, confession, prayer and discipline by meeting almost daily. Through the leaders of the choirs, Zinzendorf helped to oversee each individual's Christian growth. From within these small groups, missionary teams were sent throughout the entire world establishing new small group communities whose purpose was reconciling others to God and to each other in community.

One of the people most influenced by Zinzendorf was John Wesley. Wesley had already been involved in a small group as a young Christian at Oxford University. Wesley described his small group experience at the university in the following way:

> I know no other place under heaven, where I can have some [friends] always at hand, of the same judgement, and engaged in the same studies; persons who are awakened into a full conviction, that they have but one work to do upon earth; who see at a distance what that one work is, even the recovery of a single eye and a clean heart; who, in

order to do this, have, according to their power, absolutely devoted themselves to God, and follow after their Lord, denying themselves, and taking up their cross daily. To have even a small number of such friends constantly watching over my soul, and administering, as need is, reproof or advice with all plainness and gentleness, is a blessing I know not where to find in any part of the kingdom. (*The Journal of John Wesley,* December 10, 1734)

Through his own small group experience at Oxford University and his exposure to the small group community at Hernhutt, John Wesley extensively incorporated small groups within his missionary work in the United States in the mid-1700s. As a result of his work, Christian small groups sprang up on such campuses as Princeton, William and Mary, the University of Pennsylvania and Brown. Christian student small groups were major forces in the spiritual awakenings of the 1790s and mid-1800s.

Small groups remained a vital vehicle for ministry on the college campus in the 1800s at places such as Cambridge University in England and Williams College in Massachusetts. As we approach the 21st century, there are thousands of small groups on college campuses throughout the entire world, products of the communities established by people such as Zinzendorf and Wesley.

Unlike previous years when small groups were predominantly located on college campuses, small groups today permeate God's church as well. In China the church survives and even thrives because of the thousands of house churches. In Korea the extraordinary growth in the church has come about primarily through small group ministry. Within the Catholic Church in Latin America small group "base communities" are a major force in spiritual renewal.

Although small group communities are varied in their formats, many groups follow a model which is based on the groups that were started by the apostles in the early church. It is this model that InterVarsity has adopted in its fellowships.

A Model for Small Group Community

Following Jesus' prayer for them in John 17, the disciples began to

"I've asked Peter to give each of you a copy of this week's discussion questions."

fulfill Jesus' goal for them, the establishment of reconciled communities. As a result of Peter's Pentecost speech, the church in Jerusalem grew in one day from 120 people (Acts 1:15) to over 3,000 people (2:41). How were all these people who had just believed in Christ as Savior and Lord going to grow in their faith and become agents of reconciliation for the gospel? They could no longer effectively continue to meet only in large groups.

As God had directed Moses during the exodus to divide his people into small units of tens and fifties, so God also led the early church to meet in smaller units. In Acts 2:46 we see that the Jerusalem church was divided into two mutually supportive meetings—a large group meeting which expressed their corporate unity ("meeting together in the temple courts") and more intimate small group meetings ("breaking of bread in homes"). The smaller units were most likely composed of individuals who lived close to one another and who met together in each other's homes. In 2:42-47 we catch a glimpse of what characterized these small group communities.

They devoted themselves to the apostles' teaching and to the fellowship, to the breaking of bread and to prayer. Everyone was filled with awe, and many wonders and miraculous signs were done by the apostles. All the believers were together and had everything in common. Selling their possessions and goods, they gave to anyone as he had need. Every day they continued to meet together in the temple courts. They broke bread in their homes and ate together with glad and sincere hearts, praising God and enjoying the favor of all the people. And the Lord added to their number daily those who were being saved.

Within this portion of Scripture we can distinguish four characteristics or components of these small groups: (1) community, (2) nurture, (3) worship and prayer, and (4) outreach. These components are central to our groups today, as they were in the first Christian small groups.

Components of a Small Group

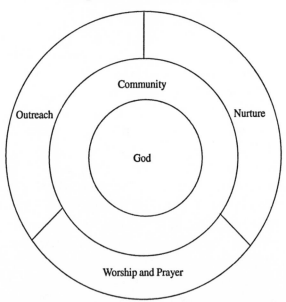

Each of these components will play a part in your group, but at different times in the life of the group you may find yourself emphasizing different areas. As the group begins, the natural focus is building community as you get to know one another. Once you are more comfortable with each other, you'll begin to worship and pray together with greater freedom. Nurture will always play a part in your group, but once you get to know each other, you'll experience community during the Bible study and prayer times, rather than through special activities. And, although outreach will be a part of the group's vision from the start, that too is something that may become a stronger focus once the group is more unified.

Don't feel that *each* meeting needs to include all of these components. What you do during the small group's time together will vary from week to week and evolve over the group's life. Each of the components will find a natural place.

Community

God's intention is for community to be the core of the church and the center of small group life (just as it's the center of the chart on p. 32). Too often our understanding of community or fellowship is superficial and limited, and we think of community as a subjective feeling of belonging. For the small groups of the early church, however, community is characterized by three specific expressions of deep unity.

First, community is *sharing together.* All Christians possess in common the objective blessings of the gospel. What should draw Christians together is not just warm feelings of togetherness, but also the concrete fact that we all share in God's grace (Philippians 1:7) through Christ. We are united with Christ and each other through Christ's death, resurrection and glory (Romans 6:3-4). Not only are we pardoned through Christ for our rebellion against God, but we are also elevated to the status of sons and daughters and thus have community with God. We have a common inheritance. This naturally leads to the component of worship and prayer.

Another expression of community is *sharing with one another.* When one was in need, the others were most willing to meet that need (Acts 2:44-45). We see further evidence of this sharing in Acts 4:32: "All the believers were one in heart and mind. No one claimed that any of his possessions was his own, but they shared everything they had." When this loving relationship developed in the early church, these small groups became groups of close, mutually concerned members, caring for each other. They had a love for each other that the world could not match.

The final expression of community, *sharing outward together* in common service, leads to the fourth component, outreach. The common inheritance which the group shares should be given out to others. The community helps its members become reconciled to God through the nurture and worship and prayer components of the small group. It is through outreach that the community of believers are involved in helping those who are alienated from God to be reconciled with him.

Nurture

The second component of small groups in the early church was nurture. This new small group community developed its reconciliation with God through devoting "themselves to the apostles' teaching" (Acts 2:42). But the early church did not merely learn about God's truth. They submitted themselves to the authority of the teaching. The result of this nurturing was a response of awe toward God (v. 43). Awe is a proper fear or respect for God which leads to worship and submission.

The equivalent of the apostles' teaching for us is the Bible. Like the early church, our small group communities should have a hunger to study God's Word and a willingness to submit to its authority, which leads to worship of God and obedience to what he commands.

Worship and Prayer

Worship and prayer make up the third component of small groups in the early church. Their worship was both formal (in the temple courts) and informal (in the homes) (Acts 2:46). Their attitude in worship was one of glad and sincere hearts which praised God (vv. 46-47) in song and prayer. As they began to understand the Scriptures and saw all that God had done for them, they responded in thanksgiving to God. Beginning to comprehend all God desired of them, they banded together in corporate prayer, asking God to change them to be more like Jesus and to change their neighbors who were not believers to receive Jesus as their Savior and Lord.

Outreach

As an expression of their community, as a result of their nurturing, out of their worship and prayer, and in spite of the intense persecution they faced, the early church small groups reached out to others. Part of this outreach meant sharing material possessions with those in need. "Do not forget to do good and to share with others, for with such sacrifices God is pleased" (Hebrews 13:16).

These small group communities extended beyond themselves not only through doing good deeds but also by bringing good news. Part of the outreach of these small groups was to call others to obedience in Jesus Christ. The results were amazing. "The Lord added to their number daily those who were being saved" (Acts 2:47).

Why did the early church experience such rapid growth? We get a clue in Acts 2:47, which states the early church enjoyed "the favor of all the people." When people from the outside looked in, they saw that this new community was different. They saw that these small groups were marked by a love of God, love for one another and a love for those who were not members. Jesus promised that Christians' love for one another would lead people to himself (John 13:35). The response by those who were not Christians was positive because they saw Christ's love for them demonstrated in these small group communities.

God's Plan for Groups

From creation until today, God has placed his people into small group communities. Although, like small groups today, these early church communities had their problems, they had unique qualities that serve as a model for 21st century groups. Elton Trueblood in *The Incendiary Fellowship* sums up the essence of small groups: "The church is consciously inadequate persons who gather because they are weak and scatter to serve because unity with each other and Christ has made them bold." May Christ make you bold as you seek to draw people into a reconciling community of nurture, worship and prayer, and outreach.

Understanding the Chapter
Study

1. Read Genesis 2:15—3:13. What is God's desire for community?

2. How did that community collapse?

Reflect

1. How did Jesus re-create us into community?

2. On a scale of 1 to 10, rate the quality of the community within your small group this past year.

Why did you rate it this way?

3. Which of the four components was strongest in your small group this year? Why?

Which was weakest? Why?

Apply

For each of the four components list one step you want to take in your group this year to improve that component.

------

[1]Some of the ideas for this part of the chapter came from Gareth Icenogle's *Biblical Foundations for Small Group Ministry.*

PART 2
SETTING OUR COURSE

3/Building Relationships: Community

4/Developing Disciples: Nurture

5/Adoring God: Worship & Prayer

6/Becoming Witnesses: Outreach

"CHIEF? COME IN, CHIEF. M°CULLEY HERE. THEY DON'T DRINK OR SMOKE AND THEY'VE NEVER EVEN HEARD OF ROCK & ROLL...SO WHAT DO I TELL THEM?"

Taken from *Faith in Orbit* © 1995 by Mary Chambers and used by permission of InterVarsity Press.

3/BUILDING RELATIONSHIPS: COMMUNITY
■ Nina Thiel

I need to share with you what's been going on with me and my parents, because you're my family," Susan began. Surrounded by eighteen listening brothers and sisters in Christ, she continued: "I have been in therapy for the past several weeks because I'm finally willing to deal with the fact that my father molested me when I was a little girl. My therapist and I have decided that it's time to confront my parents, and I need you to pray for me."

Into the middle of the room she went, and we gathered around her, many praying in tears, but all praying gently for our sister and for her parents. Several weeks later, during the counseling session at which Susan did confront her parents, we gathered in an apartment near campus to pray. When Susan arrived, at first she just cried, then she told us about it, and then she thanked us for being there for her.

The core of the group Susan was in was a small group of eight students who had met together the entire year before as a regular campus small group. It was during one of the first meetings of the year the following fall that Susan asked to tell her story and requested prayer. We had not only become her spiritual family, but in some ways were functioning more effectively than the family she grew up in. She shared more intimately than many could ever imagine doing. Why? Why could she trust us in that way? Susan was a part of a community.

The Beginning of Community

Not only was Susan part of her small group community, she was also part of a larger history of God fulfilling his purposes through small group communities. For the early Christians, community was vital because they were isolated from and persecuted by society. They gathered together for mutual support and encouragement much as Susan's group did.

God also gave each of his people certain abilities or gifts. To fulfill their reconciling ministry to each other and to the world around them, the early Christians depended on each other in these small group communities. The young house church in Ephesus saw this need for interdependence in community fairly quickly.

It was he [Jesus] who gave some to be apostles, some to be prophets, some to be evangelists, and some to be pastors and teachers, to prepare God's people for works of service, so that the body of Christ may be built up until we all reach unity in the faith and in the knowledge of the Son of God and become mature, attaining to the whole measure of the fullness of Christ.

. . . From him the whole body, joined and held together by every supporting ligament, grows and builds itself up in love, as each part does its work. (Ephesians 4:11-13, 16)

In this kind of community, the whole becomes greater than the sum of its parts as all the members work together by using their gifts to help each other be reconciled to God and to each other, and to be involved in reconciling to God those people who are presently alienated from him. Susan benefited from a small group that helped her grow closer to God, learn to trust her brothers and sisters in Christ and be reconciled to her father. But her small group did not start with this level of intimacy.

The first time your small group meets, you'll probably look around the room and wonder (as Susan's small group leader did the first time her group met) how in the world this diverse, unharmonious group of people will become a true community. How will this group become a collection of people committed to each other no matter what? How will it become a safe haven where we can be vulnerable? How will this group become a place of accountability and challenge? How will it become a place of deep friendships?

Like all the other aspects of small group life, a strong sense of community won't naturally develop in your small group unless you set it as a goal and begin working toward it from the start. And it won't develop if your small group members don't participate in its growth. M. Scott Peck, in his book *The Road Less Traveled,* says, "Love is an action, an activity." Communities are made, not born.

Ingredients for Community-Making

1. Unity in Christ. There are lots of communities made up of people who don't know Jesus at all. If we believe the gospel, we believe that the deepest communities are spiritual in connection, and the deepest spiritual connection with each other is ultimately only available in our relationship with Jesus Christ, our Redeemer and Lord. In him is recognition of our sin and profound need for forgiveness and healing; in him is restoration and regeneration; in him is the call to link arms as brothers and sisters to reach the world with the gospel.

Though many small groups will include those who haven't yet given their lives to Jesus, with other Christians in your group you will have a common commitment to Christ and his mission to the world. That link is a powerful one, because it's

Overheard in a Community-less Small Group

1. "What was your name again?"
2. "Well, since no one has any prayer requests . . ."
3. "Did anyone meet with their one-on-one last week?"
4. "Well, since it looks like no one else is coming, let's just forget it for this week."
5. "I'm just here for the Bible study. I already have friends."

attached at our cores. Talk about a head start! As Christians, we're already "members of one another" (Romans 12:5 NRSV).

I'll never forget my small group at a two-year community college. It was made up of three skateboarders from the local nondenominational church, an ex-Catholic nun, a woman with purple hair, a thirty-nine year-old divorced mother of two, a couple of "normal" collegians and me. Other than the fact that all except me were students, we had nothing in common—except that we all knew Jesus and wanted to follow him. What I remember most is the way we studied the Scriptures together and prayed for each other. Our unity in Christ drew us together faster than anything else could.

2. Shared experiences. Bonding is what happens when a mother and father hold their child for the first time. Bonding is what happens when missionaries spend time with and befriend nationals in their new home as soon as they arrive. Bonding is what happens when you find a puppy, carry it all the way home, feed it, love it and beg your parents to let you keep it. We will bond with our small group members, and they will bond with us and with each other if we spend time together early and often.

At first we, as the leaders, will take a lot of initiative in bringing the group together. From gathering for the fellowship's beginning-of-the-year ice-cream social to dinners together in the first or second week (or almost nightly if you're in a residence hall) to planning from the start to go together to the fellowship's fall conference to sitting together at large group meetings—early experiences link people together and provide a context for deeper sharing and just plain old getting to know each other.

To all of the above activities, Susan's small group added commitment to outreach, planning and going together on a week-long mission in another culture. That particular shared experience did more to unite them than a week at the beach. So, while going for coffee or yogurt is a lot better than nothing, sharing experiences with built-in content—like conferences, special workshops or extra time in Scripture—is even better than that.

As a leader, make it a practice to take your members along with you wherever you go—the grocery store, an impromptu football game with other members of the fellowship, church and more. Soon they'll be rounding up each other. Hopefully, they'll remember to include you!

3. Trust and vulnerability. The goal of many small group exercises is to allow for self-disclosure in a nonthreatening way. Especially when your small group first begins meeting together, you'll want to plan some of these to help people get to know each other and get used to sharing about themselves. Well-planned community-building activities can teach people to become a part of each other's lives. Here are some tips (see *Small Group Idea Book* for actual ideas):

☐ Fun is good. Games are good. Drawing is good. Laughing is good. All those things are relaxing and safe for most people. Be creative in finding ways to help your members tell about themselves.

☐ Meaningful is good. Telling your favorite salad dressing, ice-cream flavor or brand of toothpaste won't help anyone know your heart; these activities are best as icebreakers. Make sure your creative activities get at the content of the lives of the people involved—from how their week really was to what gives them the most joy in following Jesus to what enables them to trust others.

☐ Sensitivity is good. Remember that your members are coming from a variety of backgrounds. Some may be embarrassed or even angry about their family of origin or events in their past. These are things they'll need to talk about as the group grows closer, but if you sense some serious panic over participating in the activity you've introduced, by all means let them sit it out. You can ask them what's up in a safer, private conversation later.

☐ Leaders must model openness. We should go first . . . and remember that only rarely will members go deeper than we do. We have to show them it's okay to reveal deeper things about ourselves. By not laughing, looking embarrassed or horrified, or changing the subject, we show how to respond when others take the risk.

Another way to develop trust and vulnerability is by setting up one-on-one meetings right away: leaders with members and members with each other. Match people up and give them something to do when they meet together. They might answer some questions about themselves, make a list of small group outings or small group outreach ideas, study a section of Scripture before the next small group meeting, or just go for coffee and talk about what happened that week. Encourage them to pray for each other, too, and model doing it in your one-on-ones. A few weeks into the semester, after everyone's had the chance to get to know each other, you could help them match up into ongoing prayer partnerships.

When my small group started last fall, I arranged time alone with Angela right away, because I knew enough about her to know she wouldn't feel comfortable in our small group until she knew at least one person better. She was happy to open up to me one-on-one, and gradually she learned to do it with our whole small group. This year, she's learning to help others open up as a small group co-leader.

As time goes on, be ready to tailor community-building activities to match the group's level of trust and vulnerability. Often, by the end of the first semester or quarter, we're finished with the games and ready to simply express prayer needs or struggles, to apply what we're studying in Scripture and to pray together for each other. When a new student in one of my husband's small groups told the group he was really homesick and wanted to know if they would pray for him, Larry knew his group had rounded a significant corner. At this point, community becomes less contrived and more natural, like driving a stick-

Four Barriers to Community

1. Time constraints. All those jobs, classes and study sessions have to go somewhere. Relationships are hard to schedule, so they often end up neglected.
2. Individuality. When we're taught to look out for number one, it's hard to "look not only to your own interests, but also to the interests of others" (Philippians 2:4).
3. Brokenness. The trust necessary to build community is weak to nonexistent in those whose families have been a lot less than healthy. The many people with divorced parents have a huge obstacle to overcome. Abuse of any kind makes trusting almost perilous.
4. Immaturity. It takes some students a good year or two before they really understand (and commit to) the value of community. And before they do, they don't know they aren't. Much grace, patience and persistence is required.

shift with a fair amount of ease, because we've all worked at building it together.

4. Accountability and Commitment. Because so many of us grew up "on our own" with self-sufficiency not only grasped by necessity but encouraged as a value, very few people understand their interconnectedness with those around them. We aren't willing to make commitments to others or to ask for, give and receive accountability in the midst of struggles. We aren't aware of the benefits of commitment.

At the same time almost everyone coming to a small group is hoping for those deep relationships in which we're really seeking to help each other grow. Sometimes it seems to me that we want the results of accountability and commitment without the sometimes difficult effort they require.

Here's how I (and some of the fellowships I've been a part of) have worked at developing accountability and commitment in small groups throughout the year:

☐ Assuming that developing close relationships is a common goal for people joining a small group, I don't hesitate to encourage commitment to the group from day one. The reasoning I give is simple: if we're going to feel comfortable with each other and feel safe talking honestly with each other, we all need to be here every week. (On a commuter campus where you're not likely to see each other much in between small group meetings, getting to the weekly meeting is especially crucial.) I also mention that it's only an hour and a half once a week that I'm asking for initially and ask members to put it in their schedules like they do their classes and

Top Five Excuses for Missing Small Group

5 I didn't feel led to attend.

4 My horoscope said it was a bad idea.

3 There was a *Star Trek* marathon weekend on TV.

2 I was busy praying about apathy in our fellowship.

1 I had a visitation from God and lost track of time.

Adapted from *The Potluck Hall of Fame* © 1991 by David Dickerson and used by permission of InterVarsity Press.

other "essentials." I usually don't even have to get into a discussion about priorities and what it really means to make Jesus number one in your life.

☐ If someone misses the meeting, I don't hesitate to call them to tell them we missed them and what we did that night, and then find out where they were and encourage them to come back. If the problem becomes chronic, I would take one-on-one time with them to go over their schedule and help them choose faithfulness to their small group.

☐ I encourage people who think they might need to miss the small group to call me or my co-leader, not to announce that they won't be coming, but to tell about the possible conflict in schedule and ask for suggestions. Sometimes the conflict is unavoidable, such as sickness, a family obligation planned months before or a choir performance. Most of the time, with a little effort the conflict can be taken care of. An appointment with a faculty advisor can be rescheduled. They can study for the exam in the afternoon instead of watching soap operas. They can plan to leave right after small group to meet their study group. The whole group could go to the choir concert. It's hard to think of alternatives alone, so having members call up to get help rather than simply bailing on the small group makes a big difference.

☐ A small group that is growing closer will probably need the chance to talk about commitment. If someone has been gone a lot, other members should feel free to tell the person how it makes them feel. If your whole group is struggling to hang together, the first time they are all there, you should feel free to talk about how you are feeling about their lack of commitment. The purpose of this isn't to lay a guilt-trip on people, but to help them see that their choices have consequences in the lives of those around them. It's not "perfect attendance" that's affected, it's the relationships in the group. Usually, talks like this really pull a group together.

☐ Encourage accountability to each other outside of the small group meeting, not only by getting members to meet together during the rest of the week, but by teaching them to think about each other, pray for each other and ask each other how it's going. You can provide paper for them to jot down each other's prayer requests or goals for applying the passage of Scripture you studied together that night. Set the tone by asking for prayer in an area of need or asking members to hold you accountable to a commitment to greater obedience.

☐ Encourage members to open themselves up to the small group for advice and community decision-making. For example, one member of my small group was involved in an ongoing theater production that was seriously affecting his relationship with Jesus and his purity. He wondered if he should give it up. He told our small group about it and said that he was thinking of quitting. Several of us supported him, saying that it sounded like he was making the right decision. When we asked him about it the next week, he had given notice.

Other issues I've seen brought up for community input and decision-making include dating relationships, career goals, ministry opportunities, majors, club involvements, conference or retreat attendance, wedding plans, moving plans and even (for my husband and me) the timing of having children. In our culture we're so used to making decisions alone and then announcing them (the American way!) that we (1) don't realize how our decisions affect those around us and (2) miss out on the support we need to make good decisions and implement them. You, the leader, will need to set the example (are you noticing a recurring theme?), and your members will follow suit.

☐ Time: Community for the Long Haul. Several years ago, my mom attended her thirty-something-year college reunion. She told me how wonderful it was to see her dormmates again, how they could sit down and talk like no time had passed at all. These were the women she'd lived with for four years. They came in as freshmen together. They supported each other through classes, majors and relationships. They cheered each other on to careers and marriages. They shared everything.

I got to thinking that this sounded a lot like what Christian community should be. We're too quick to end relationships in which God has worked and start new ones. We start totally new small groups every year (or semester!), form leadership teams without considering the relationships of those involved and go off to find jobs after graduation wherever we can find one, rather than continuing to build relationships with others and making decisions about where to live based on the priority of community.

I began to encourage students to stay together. Possibly, they'd all be in the same small group again next year (with room for new members, of course). Maybe some would lead the group and others would be members. A strong small group could become the team of small group leaders for a certain area of campus the next year. Maybe each member would be involved in a different ministry of the fellowship but would continue to live in the same building and meet together. After graduation, small group communities from your school could continue ministering together in the marketplace, mission field, inner city or on campus.

Interview with a Small Group Leader

By now you might be thinking: "Sounds great. But is it really possible to include all those ingredients for community-building in one small group? And what does it look like day in and day out? Is all this realistic for my small group in my campus situation?" Let's hear from one small group leader (well, me!) in a normal-to-difficult situation community-building-wise and take a practical look at one small group's experience developing community.

SGLH: What has been your latest experience in small group community?

Me: I had a really good small group last year, especially considering our biggest handicap—because UNLV is a commuter campus, we met at lunchtime in a conference room in the student union. Talk about obstacles to community building!

SGLH: What did you and your co-leaders emphasize with that particular group to help make it into a family?

Me: In the "shared experiences" department, we found weekly participation in the Friday night large group meeting was our chance to hang out together. All but two (out of twelve) members went to our fellowship's Fall Conference in October—our chance to spend the whole weekend together. Most of us spent an evening together in November helping serve dinner at the Salvation Army downtown and being debriefed by one of the ministers there. This was risky for us, but really drew us together.

SGLH: How did you develop trust and vulnerability?

Me: We thought it through and planned really quality community-building activities for our first several meetings. We met with everyone in our group during the week between our first and second meetings, then began setting up one-on-ones between all the members. Because our group was on the large side as small groups go, we nearly always planned some time during our meetings to break into groups of two or three—maybe to do a community exercise, to discuss some of the major observations or personal applications from the passage we were studying, or to pray for friends we were planning to invite to the next evangelistic large group meeting. Also, as co-leaders, we were very open with each other and brought that vulnerability into our small group.

SGLH: What about accountability and commitment?

Me: From our first time together we were honest about the fact that it would be extra difficult for us to grow close to each other given our meeting time and location. We emphasized the essentialness of coming each week. We were also pretty good about calling people who missed small group. By the second semester, it hardly ever happened.

SGLH: In your chapter on community, you write about the importance of small group members considering staying together beyond a semester, year or even beyond college. We assume that section probably has no relevance for a small group like yours because of the highly transitory commuter situation.

Me: Actually, it has a lot of relevance. Schedules always change between semesters. We very early—before spring semester schedules came out— began encouraging our members to keep our meeting time free for the next semester. All but one did. And he immediately joined another group at a nonconflicting time. It also helped that one of my co-leaders plus two of our members had been in my small group—same time, same location— the year before. We brought continuity and experience with us.

SGLH: Well, how did this small group turn out?

Me: Really good! Some of the women in the group met together for deeper study, accountability and prayer. Five of us went to Urbana. One went on a summer mission. One is overseas for a year teaching English. Five of the remaining ten students are on the leadership team of the fellowship—two of them leading that noon-in-the-student-union small group this year. Everybody grew closer to Jesus and to each other.

Putting It all Together

I began this chapter with the story of Susan. Three years later, Susan is still a part of the same team of leaders that grew out of her small group. Yes, new ones have become part of the team and others have graduated from "official" involvement, but the community has continued. As they near graduation, members of that original group are asking themselves how they can continue ministering together. One couple, already graduated and married, chose to stay in town, look for jobs there and lead a small group on campus as alumni volunteers. The others are finishing up and thinking ahead with "life together" as a consideration if not a priority. And my husband and I, in our own decision-making process for the future, won't entertain any option unless community members are involved. Community, once formed, is too valuable to us and too useful for the kingdom to lose.

Understanding the Chapter
Study

1. Read Philippians 1:1-11. What words and phrases reveal the feelings and the unity of Paul and the Philippian believers?

2. What does Paul hope for them?

3. How could God use a small group to accomplish the goals found in these verses?

Reflect

1. Think about the people you're closest to. How have each of the elements mentioned in the chapter (unity in Christ, shared experiences, trust and vulnerability, accountability and commitment, and time) contributed to the building of those relationships?

2. Think about your current small group. Which of the elements is your group's strength? weakness?

3. How can you work on the weaknesses in your group?

4. Almost everything in the chapter required the small group leader to

"set the tone" in order to lead a small group into community. What elements will be or are difficult for you to model? Why?

5. What or who could help you be better prepared for intimacy and commitment in your small group as its leader?

Apply

1. Start by writing down the answer to this question: At the end of the year, in our relationships with each other, our small group will be a group of people who _____

_____

_____ .

You probably won't meet your goal in the first month of your small group's life, but you can get off to a good start.

2. Plan the community activities for the first four weeks of your small group, keeping a balance of all the "ingredients for community-making."

4/DEVELOPING DISCIPLES: NURTURE
■ Patty Pell

We met in the basement of Tobey-Kendal Hall. The TV was turned off, and we gathered in a circle on the run-down couches and torn-up carpet. We were a mixed group of new students, seniors, education majors, music majors, quiet souls and outgoing personalities. A Bible lay on each person's lap opened to the book of Romans. As we read and studied God's Word, the truths that we saw transformed us as individuals and as a group. Sometimes we struggled to understand, and sometimes we sat in awe. But each time we met God.

One of the reasons we gather in small groups is to grow as disciples. A primary way we do this is through Bible study. We understand what it means to follow Christ more each time we are in the Word.

In Luke 6:46-49 Jesus tells about two kinds of builders—those who build their houses on the rock and those who build without a foundation—to emphasize what happens to us when we hear his words and obey and what happens when we ignore his words.

Why do you call me, "Lord, Lord," and do not do what I say? I will show you what he is like who comes to me and hears my words and puts them into practice. He is like a man building a house, who dug down deep and laid a foundation on rock. When a flood came, the torrent struck that house but could not shake it, because it was well built. But the one who hears my words and does not put them into practice is like a man who built a house on the ground without a foundation. The moment the torrent struck that house, it collapsed and its destruction was complete.

Two elements in this story give us insight as to why studying Scripture is so crucial. One is that a wise person must *hear God's words*. We must study the Bible so that we know what God has revealed to us and how he desires us to live. The second thought is that hearing must lead to *putting God's words into practice*. Knowing the Bible does not alone make us disciples. It is the application of God's truths that transforms us and glorifies him. This is not easy, but by studying the Scriptures with others our understanding of God's Word is enhanced, and our ability to act in obedience to what we have learned is also strengthened.

Hearing God's Words

How do we know who God is? How do we determine what truth is? How do we find out how to act and live? How has God worked in the world, and how does he interact with his people? The answer to all these questions is *Scripture*. It holds the record of God's work, the revelation of God. It is in the pages of Scripture that we hear the words of Jesus and watch him love and touch people. It is in the pages of Scripture that we witness the people of Israel learning to be God's people. It is here that we first learn the good news, and it is here that we learn to pray. Scripture is our final authority.

But Scripture is more than a textbook. Hebrews 4:12 describes it this way: "For the word of God is living and active. Sharper than any double-edged sword, it penetrates even to dividing soul and spirit, joints and marrow; it judges the thoughts and attitudes of the heart." We are changed when we study Scripture. The Holy Spirit works in us to convict us of areas of our hearts and lives that are not in line with what we are reading. It is often when we are reading Scripture that we are overwhelmed by the truth in it and are moved to action. It is the truths in Scripture that keep us from being consumed by the world's views of life. Psalm 1:1-2 reminds us "Happy are those who do not follow the advice of the wicked . . . but their delight is in the law of the LORD" (NRSV).

WHEN BIBLE TRANSLATIONS GET OUT OF HAND

Taken from *It Came from Beneath the Pew* © 1989 by Rob Suggs and used by permission of InterVarsity Press.

The Word of God is not only our authority in matters of faith and practice. It not only moves us to confession and action. Studying the Word permeates our souls with the joy of the Lord. As we are filled with the perspective of the Almighty, our souls are put at rest. It is no wonder then that we must continually immerse ourselves in the study of Scripture and our small groups must be guided and grounded in Bible study. This is the hearing of which Jesus speaks in Luke 6.

To hear the words of God we must understand them. And to understand often requires the insight of others. Small groups provide us a wonderful setting in which to truly hear the words of God. We discuss, add our thoughts and opinions, and wrestle with what we read.

Putting God's Words into Practice
If we are wise builders once we have heard God's words, we will put them

into practice. When Jesus tells the story of the wise and foolish builders in Luke 6, he is in the company of the disciples and a crowd of other people. He begins his story by questioning everyone who calls him "Lord"; some are refusing to obey what he has commanded. The important part for Jesus is not that his disciples have great volumes of knowledge stored away in their minds but that they do what he says.

Practice as inward change. We can study Scripture for years to gain knowledge about God and about the life of faith. But God is not interested in how much we know if it has no effect on our hearts and lives. Romans 12:2 says "be transformed by the renewing of your mind." The Lord wants to see his people changed beginning with their hearts and including their behavior. The goal of Bible study is not just to memorize verses but to let verses change our attitudes and actions.

Application must begin in the transformation of our hearts. Too often when we study Scripture, we reach the end of a study and focus on the one or two things that we can do to apply the lesson from the passage. This is part of application, but we will not be able to maintain the change in behavior if our hearts have not been transformed first. As we study Scripture, we must allow it to eat away at the areas of our insides which are displeasing and worldly. As we are renewed, godly actions will follow.

Practice as outward change. At church my small group had been studying how to care for those inside and outside the group in practical ways. As we studied, we began to see God's heart for people, and our desire to care for each other grew. Thankfully the transforming process did not end there. People in the group began to do special things for each other. When our daughter was born, we received meals every day for a week from our small group. Later, we took meals to a new mother in the community whom we had met through a church outreach. We helped some group members move and others to paint their house. We planned going away parties and welcome home parties.

Can you imagine what our campuses would look like if we all put into practice everything we read in our Bibles on a daily basis? Our lives would be a living sacrifice and fragrant offering to the Lord, and those around us would be drawn to the Father in great numbers.

Practice as community. Small groups are an ideal place to put God's words into practice. As a community, we begin to understand the commands of Christ through Bible study, and the group itself acts as the context to encourage and maintain application through accountability, prayer and support. We are not strong enough on our own to obey the words we read in Scripture, so the Lord gives us strength many times through the relationships around us, including our small group.

Not only do we need the context of relationships in order to apply God's truth, but we also become a great light to the world around us when our community reflects Christ. When our small group begins to live like the early church in Acts 2:42-47—where the believers shared everything they had with one another, prayed together and fellowshiped together—the world will take notice.

Becoming Wise People

Carol shifts uncomfortably in her chair and stares again at the open page of her Bible. She doesn't quite understand the question. It doesn't seem to fit with what she feels the passage is saying. Jane, the leader, is struggling to get anyone in the group to say anything. Carol can tell the leader is uncomfortable too, but doesn't know what to do. Jane begins talking to fill the silence.

Hon shakes himself back into attention. His mind has been wandering uncontrollably since they started looking at the passage. He has been having trouble concentrating on what Jane has been saying. Jane talks on about her view of the passage. Hon has lost track of whether they are on point four or five now. He wonders if any of the other members of his small group have had a chance to say anything. He catches a peek at his watch.

I imagine everyone has been in situations similar to those of the people above. And as we think about leading, we may wonder if our group will be any different. Let's take a look at the specifics of planning and leading a solid Bible study.

There are two ways of looking at a passage of Scripture—deductively and inductively. To approach a passage deductively means that you rea-

CLIFTON'S TATTOO WAS BIBLICALLY ACCURATE, AND MADE A FINE CONVERSATION PIECE AS WELL.

son from the general to the specific. You begin by suggesting a hypothesis, such as "Jesus is compassionate." Then you go about proving this statement with the passage in question. Although the statement is true, the passage may not be making this particular point. Thus, deductive methods oftentimes cause a group to miss the point of a passage or even misinterpret the passage's meaning.

Inductive Bible study, on the other hand, is a method of reasoning which moves from the particular to the general. You approach a passage and look at all the specifics contained in it. Then you put those together to end with a general statement about the passage's meaning. For instance, a group reads a passage and looks at all the details. After the group puts the specifics together, they decide that Jesus must be compassionate. By looking at what is in the passage first there is a better chance that a group or individual will come close to the author's original intent. Because we are more likely to understand the meaning of a passage more clearly if we study it inductively, this is the best method for small groups. However, there are other reasons to use this method.

My high-school English teacher frequently gave us a strange assignment. We were instructed to read a certain poem, piece of prose or play and then bring to class at least five questions that we had about our reading. We were given a grade for bringing in our questions. It did not matter what they were, only that we had them. I never fully understood the reason for such an assignment until I began to study Scripture more seriously. In writing those questions we were forced to look deeper into the poem or prose, trying to discover what the meanings were and the connections between things. Writing questions awakened in us a desire for discovery which heightened our desire to learn.

We understand more fully and are more excited about learning when we are given the opportunity to discover a certain truth rather than simply having someone explain it to us. There is an old proverb which captures this truth: "I hear, I forget. I see, I remember. When I do, I understand."

One final reason the inductive method is so crucial to our study of Scripture is the way it teaches people to study the Bible on their own. These valuable study skills will be a source of wisdom for the group members for the rest of their lives.

Steps to Inductive Bible Study

If you can master just three steps, you can study Scripture, prepare a Bible study, teach others inductive methods and be on your way to facilitating a good small group discussion. The key words are *observation, interpretation* and *application,* three steps we use in all areas of our lives.

Observation is gathering the facts. It is answering the *who, what, when, where* questions. Observation is something we automatically do every day. For example, Sherri goes to class for the first time and notices many things in that hour. She sees a wide mix of students from other countries in the class. The class is very small, and the professor is dressed very neatly. She might observe from the syllabus that there are many long reading assignments and papers due and that the class is made up of juniors and seniors.

Another example is Mario, who drives into town for the first time. He has the address of his friend's apartment on a piece of paper on the dashboard. As he drives north through town he is aware that he is passing 13th Street, 14th Street, 15th Street and so on. He turns to go west and realizes that he is now passing 23rd Avenue, 24th Avenue, 25th Avenue. He is gathering the facts about the town.

In Bible study we gather facts like: Who is involved in the passage? Where does the story take place? To whom is the letter written? What were the circumstances of the setting? What was said? How did a certain person behave?

Observation is the most frequently skipped step in Bible study. We have a tendency to read a passage and jump directly into interpretation or even application. What we must remember is that in order to understand what a passage means we must first observe what is there. Observation will be the most difficult part of Bible study to train your small group to do, but it is a key step if we want to honor Scripture and the Holy Spirit.

Interpretation is drawing meaning and significance from the details. When Sherri begins to draw meaning from what she observes her first day of class, she concludes that because there are so many upperclass students in the small-size class and the syllabus is full of assignments, it may be a difficult course. Mario is also beginning to interpret the facts. He learns that the layout of the city is a grid where all the streets running east-west are numbered streets and the streets running north-south are numbered avenues. Glancing at his piece of paper, he figures out where his friend's apartment can be found.

Interpreting Scripture is answering the *how* and *why* questions. It requires taking all the observations, looking for connections between them, finding significance in them and asking, "What does this mean?" Interpretation is where most of the wrestling and discussion will take place in a small group Bible study. People's faces light up when they see something for the first time or understand a passage in a new way. As observations are connected together, the main theme of the passage becomes clear. We discover what the author meant. This unchanging truth is what we want to take up residence in our hearts.

An important aspect of observation and interpretation is looking at the context of the passage—how it relates to the passages before and after it as well as the historical and cultural situation. Marking observations about these areas aids us significantly in understanding what the author was trying to communicate.

The third step is a smooth transition from meaning into action, whether the action is an inward change or an outward one—application. It is answering the *So what?* or the *What now?* questions and the question "What is the significance of this passage to you?" This is the place in Bible study where you begin to think and talk about how the passage affects you and what it will mean in your own life. Is there something in this passage to affirm, avoid or accomplish in your life? Although the meaning of a passage doesn't change, the application or the significance of the passage to individual lives may vary from person to person.

Application is integral to our study of Scripture. If Mario discovers exactly where his friend lives and then does not use that information, he will never reach the apartment, and his observations and interpretations will have been in vain. In the same way, if Sherri understands that the class will be difficult, but makes no change in her study habits to prepare for the extra work, she will receive no benefit from her discovery.

Application does not end after everyone answers the last question and leaves the meeting room; it goes with each person into all of life. And the community plays a key role, because we need each other in order to live out the truths of Scripture. As Dietrich Bonhoeffer put it: "The Christian needs another Christian who speaks God's word to him. He needs him again and again when he becomes uncertain and discouraged, for by himself he cannot help himself without belying the truth."

Planning the Bible Study

Jen sits down with her Bible to begin preparing for her small group meeting. She is excited about the passage the group will discuss this week; it is one of her favorites. She digs into the passage she has chosen, attempting to observe, interpret and apply on her way to writing her own study questions.

Across the country, Steve walks into the library to prepare for his small group. He opens his backpack, pulls out his Bible and a study guide on the book of Romans. He begins his work of putting together his study from his own preparation and the guide's questions.

On another campus Maria pulls out her colored pencils and typed pages with the Luke text. She prepares for her small group study by using the manuscript study method to glean every drop of truth from the Gospel of Luke.

On yet another campus Grace walks into a room full of small group leaders. They gather together every week to pray and prepare their Bible studies. They prep as a team and work on the questions together with their staffworkers.

Each of these leaders will lead well-written inductive studies. No matter what method of preparation your fellowship uses, there are pointers you need to know about each one.

Writing Your Own Bible Study
Step 1: Studying the Passage

Observation. Read the passages before and after your particular text to get a feel for the entire section. This will help you understand the author's intent in writing your passage and how it fits into the whole section's theme. Reading the passage in context will greatly enhance your understanding of the passage. To really gain the larger perspective it is also helpful to read the entire book you are working in.

Another very important part of the overview is to do some reading about the historical and cultural context or background of your passage. Find out what the times were like, what the setting was, how peo-

Using Manuscript Studies

One way of challenging your small group is to use manuscript studies. A manuscript is the biblical text typed without any verse markings, chapter designations, paragraphs or notes. Each person uses different colored pencils or markers to designate repeated and contrasting words, phrases and ideas, as well as any cause and effect statements. Each person spends time observing in the text and connecting the words on the pages with the colored pencils: for example, blue for repetition, red for contrasts, and green for cause and effect. Discussion takes place when the group members tell what they have found and begin to try to find meaning from their connections. Manuscript is a fun, hands-on way of doing inductive Bible study.

ple did things during this period. An extremely helpful tool in discovering some of the rich cultural background is the *New Bible Dictionary* (IVP).

Then work through your passage, making observations such as who the characters are, where the events occur, what is taking place, what is being said. Go deeper with your observations by finding repeated words or phrases, contrasting words or ideas, or other interesting ideas that stand out.

Interpretation. Next answer the "why" questions. Find the meanings of the repetitions you found. Ask yourself why things happened a certain way or why someone said something. Determine the main point of the passage.

Application. Ask what the central theme means to you. What attitudes, thoughts, relationships or actions does it require changing?

Step 2: Writing the Study

Purpose. Write down what you want to see accomplished in the course of your discussion. This may be something you want your group members to understand, become aware of or do.

Introduction. Write an opening or approach question that exposes a need and gets group members thinking about the issues that will arise in the study.

Questions. Take the observations, interpretations and applications you've made and turn those into questions. Write several questions from each category. Good questions are ones that require people to give several answers from the text, not just a yes or no. These open-ended questions will facilitate good discussion and allow several people to answer. The final application question can refer back to the opening question to tie the study together. If you want the group to respond with some action, make sure the application question addresses this.

Evaluation. Make sure the questions flow from one to another and accomplish your purpose. Ask yourself: Are my questions brief and clear? Do they make the group search the text and move through the passage? Does each question point toward the central theme? Do the application questions lead the group to specific actions? Try to be aware of how long your study will take. A good length is about 10-12 questions. Make sure that within your ten questions you have several observation, several interpretation and two or so application questions.

Using a Bible Study Guide
Step 1: Choosing a Guide
Upon entering a Christian bookstore and finding the study guide section, you will be inundated with all kinds of study guides which cover the spectrum of topics and Bible books. There are guides which require outside work, guides which look at many different verses and passages in each study, guides that focus on one passage, and guides which are fill-in-the-blank. How do you know which guides are best?

1. Choose guides that do not require preparation before the meeting. These are difficult in groups with open membership.

2. Find guides that primarily stay in one passage at a time. These give members a better understanding of inductive Bible study.

3. Scan the questions. Make sure that they are not one-answer questions, that they will facilitate discussion and will allow several members to answer. A good question would be something like this: "What do we learn about Samuel's character in verses 1-5?"

4. Choose guides that will not take up your entire meeting time so that you have time for the other components.

5. Gather guides that are made for small groups, not individual devotions or large groups.

The nurture section of *Small Group Idea Book* has a list of some inductive Bible study guides. Using study guides can help us learn how to write and lead solid Bible studies. They can give us valuable insight into the passage, and they can reduce the time it takes to prepare a study. However, using a guide can also tempt us to forgo our own study of the passage and show up unprepared. Using a study guide does require some preparation.

Step 2: Using the Study Guide
Preparing the study. A good place to start is to read the historical and cultural background of the book and passage that is given in the guide

to better understand the author's intent in writing the passage. Then, put the study guide aside and do your own work in the passage. Read the passage in the midst of other passages around it to get the context. Make your observations and develop interpretations. Once you have discovered the main point, begin applying it to your life. The last area to think about is your purpose: What is it that you want your group to understand or do?

Formulating the study. Now that you have spent quality time in the passage yourself, pick up the study guide. Look at the study guide author's main point and introduction to see how it fits with your own. Be willing to adjust your own thinking, perhaps, as you read through the study guide. And be sure to check the leader's notes in the back of the guide, which give you even more valuable insight into the passage.

You may want to rewrite some of the questions in your own words so you feel more comfortable with them. Try adding questions if you feel the study needs it or deleting questions which are difficult to understand. The goal is to work with the guide until you understand each question. Adding questions can be tricky, so the following ideas may help.

1. Always use clearly worded questions that facilitate discussion by asking for several answers. Avoid questions which have only one answer.

2. Make sure the added questions flow with the surrounding questions and move toward your purpose.

3. Formulate each question from your observations, interpretations or applications.

Five Ways to Kill a Discussion

1. When someone offers a far-out answer, don't respond at all; just ask the next question.

2. Always end a question with "The answer is . . . ," and then give your opinion.

3. Make sure to let only one person answer each question.

4. Whatever you do, never affirm a group member's answer. That will only lead to more input from other people.

5. Ask only questions that require yes or no answers from the group; this helps the study go much faster.

Leading the Discussion

One challenge to facilitating a good Bible discussion is making the study smooth and interesting. The goal is to be so comfortable with the study and the questions that the whole group glides along from question to question. What does this look like? Let's take a peek at two different small groups and see how the leaders are doing.

When Junko asks her opening question, there is a little discussion. She waits until no one else says anything, then picks up her notes and says, "O.k., now we go to the second question." She reads the question aloud, and then puts down her notes to wait for the group's response. Later in the study she remarks that the sixth question is not very good, but she'll go ahead and ask it. Along the way Junko adds some questions off the top of her head, and the group members express confusion about what she's looking for. The study is choppy, people have a difficult time connecting with it and at times feel uneasy.

Reggie asks his opening question, and then as discussion winds down goes on to the next one. Questions flow from one to the next. As the discussion continues, Reggie watches for opportunities to smoothly interject the next question. He builds on people's comments and asks relevant questions. His notes are inconspicuously set to the side of his Bible, but he just glances at them from time to time. The group feels very comfortable, the discussion is lively, and Reggie is not the center of attention.

These two groups point to some important guidelines.

Secrets of Successful Bible Study Leadership

1. At the first meeting and occasionally thereafter discuss the following principles for good Bible discussion (adapted from *Bible & Life* material) with your group:

☐ Be open to learning from the Bible.

☐ The Bible is the authority. Expect it, rather than the leader, to answer the questions that come up.

☐ To keep everyone on the same level, stay in the passage under discussion, rather than referring to other passages or bringing in commentaries and other references.

☐ Stay on the point under discussion.

2. Decide what you want the group members to learn and keep moving toward that purpose.

3. Be creative with an introductory question that will get the group thinking.

4. Know your questions well and avoid calling attention to them.

5. Try to avoid moving to the next question by always adding your input to the question. It may seem that you are giving the "correct" answer each time before moving on to the next question. However, summarizing what has been contributed by members can be helpful.

6. Build on what others say during the discussion. You might ask another question which naturally flows from someone's answer to clarify and show that you are listening.

7. Allow a sufficient time of silence for people to think before you rephrase the question.

8. Try to make transitions between questions smooth so the study flows together.

9. Be aware of how members are doing even during the study. For instance, if a usually talkative person rarely talks one week, maybe there is something wrong.

10. Watch for what God is doing in the group during the study and be sure to listen to the Holy Spirit.

Let me encourage you that it takes a great deal of practice and experience to lead a solid Bible discussion. If you are having great difficulty, it may help to ask your small group coordinator or your staffworker to drop in on your small group meeting and then give you some feedback. It helps to have another person's perspective sometimes. Another helpful approach is to go over the guidelines for groups found in chapter eight (pp. 123-25) with the small group in one of the first meetings.

God uses us as we grow and learn. We will never know all there is to know about leading or always have wonderfully smooth discussions. We can only prepare, pray and work at developing our skills over time. However, if we care about all the members in our group and their ideas, they will respond to us as leaders.

Understanding the Chapter
Study

1. Look at Psalm 19:7-11. How are the Scriptures described?
What do they accomplish?

2. How has studying Scripture with a small group created some of these same effects in your own life?

Reflect

1. How does being in a small group help us hear, understand and apply Scripture?

2. What were the problems with Junko's study?
How could she correct them?

Apply

1. Study John 1:35-51. Using the principles outlined in this chapter, write two observation questions, two interpretation questions and two application questions.

2. Write a purpose statement and an opening question for this passage.

3. If possible, practice leading your study with a small group.

5/ADORING GOD: WORSHIP & PRAYER
■ Ann Beyerlein

During my sophomore year in college, it was obvious that Dave was getting close to asking me out. He was a great person but somewhat older, and I wasn't sure I wanted a romantic relationship. Often when he talked to me, I know I looked uncomfortable, gave no eye contact and answered in a brief monotone. I treated him like the invisible man. Finally, one day I ran into him in the university chapel, and it happened: he asked me for my phone number. In my confusion and nervousness, I accidentally gave him my phone number from *freshman* year. (What was I thinking?) Needless to say, I never heard from him again.

Worship and prayer is an important small group component because it involves us in humble awareness and conversation with God. Unfortunately, however, our prayer lives sometimes function about as well as my sophomore-year communication skills. God is talking to us through his Word, and he desires to hear from us, but our responses are often brief, rude or dishonest. We are not looking to God, which results in little awareness or vision of God's character. Sometimes, like my crazy phone number mishap, we even make it difficult for God to get through to us. This can happen in small groups when we devote little time or energy to worship and prayer and can even spill over to not listening very much to each other when we pray or give prayer requests.

As a community, we come together in worship and prayer to acknowledge and adore God's character, to respond to the Scriptures, to confess our sins, to thank God, and to bring each other's needs and the needs of our campus and world before him. In many ways worship and prayer are the heartbeat of the small group because in prayer often the nurture, community and outreach components are addressed and deepened.

In Colossians 3 Paul describes group worship and prayer in a holistic way with feelings, thoughts and actions that glorify God and spring from the Scriptures:

> Let the peace of Christ rule in your hearts, to which indeed you were called in the one body. And be thankful. Let the word of Christ dwell in you richly; teach and admonish one another in all wisdom; and with gratitude in your hearts sing psalms, hymns, and spiritual songs to God. And whatever you do, in word or deed, do everything in the name of the Lord Jesus, giving thanks to God the Father through him. (vv. 15-17 NRSV)

This chapter will discuss worship and prayer separately with separate lists of activities. However, there is definite overlap as worship includes prayer, and prayer often includes worship. On a given evening a small group may only have one prayer time that may incorporate aspects of worship.

Worshiping Together

This fall our chapter t-shirts had the slogan "Check Your Vision" on the back with characteristics of God listed underneath in decreasing size. We chose this theme because it's difficult for Christians to function effectively without a constant awareness of God's character.

Worship is essentially responding to God's character in ways that bring him honor. In a biblical sense worship involves everything we do—loving and adoring God with our heart, soul, mind and strength as in Colossians 3. Worship is an attitude, beginning with hearts that are humble and

CHECK YOUR VISION

L O V E
F A I R
P E R F E C T
I N F I N I T E
P O W E R F U L
F O R G I V I N G

reverent. Worship continues as we offer prayers of praise on our knees or as we share our faith, help the poor, or are generous with a roommate. When we do these things, we tell the world what God is like and thus declare his glory. Therefore, our personal and group prayer times are just one aspect of worshipful lives.

The goal of worship is to please God, not to have a pleasant feeling. However, when we fix our eyes on God, like Isaiah did in 40:27-31, our strength and hope are often renewed. Life comes back into perspective as we remember God's greatness, control and his unfathomable love for us. Worshiping with others often brings even greater refreshment and awareness of God's character.

What would a worshipful small group look like?

As finals week drew near, the members of a small group I was leading entered the dorm room in various emotional states. Two women were giggling incessantly, one was late and two looked depressed and preoccupied. I had to remind myself that no matter what it looked like on the outside, these women were thirsty to experience, remember and worship

God. As we ate Christmas cookies and talked about what we had learned about God that quarter, it slowly seemed like we were entering holy ground.

Our worshipful discussion helped us "see" God and make space for him in our busy lives. We sensed God unifying us. After praying together, we left renewed. Suddenly, finals, going home for Christmas and relationship issues were less overwhelming in light of God's control, goodness and power. God had reminded us of how he had sustained us for the last few months.

Although it can happen in a variety of ways, small group worship simply involves inviting each other to envision our wonderful God and enjoy being refreshed in his presence.

What kind of vision for worship should a leader have? You may be surprised to hear that it may or may not include singing! However, everything should be done in a way that would please and reflect God. For example, members should treat each other with respect because they are made in God's image and that's how God treats us. The group should handle Scripture with reverence because it is God's Word. Sin should be taken seriously in light of a holy God, and we should remind each other of God's character as we deal with problems and failures.

A leader should periodically ask, "How can we adore God and reflect his character tonight?" or "How can I help people become aware of God's character?" or "How can I remind the group that God is the Shepherd, Creator and King?" The leader might then create an activity or a time of singing or just watch for ways to address God's character and remind the group of God's presence as the group develops during a given meeting.

Small group worship should be simple, natural and focused on the one God we all worship. This unites us. Children in their honesty and expressiveness are among the best worshipers I know. In David Heller's book *Children's Letters to God* we read: "Dear God, I do not think anybody could be a better God. Well I just want you to know but I am not just saying that because you are God. Charles." This is a good example of the simple trust and love we should express to God in our worship.

In our unity as Christians, however, there is diversity in the ways we

APRIL 2015: TENSION DEVELOPS BETWEEN THOSE INSISTING ON THE TRADITIONAL DISCO WORSHIP SERVICES, AND THE YOUNGER CROWD CALLING FOR TRENDIER GRUNGE WORSHIP

Taken from Faith in Orbit © 1995 by Rob Suggs and used by permission of InterVarsity Press.

worship. On campus small groups often include people from different cultural and denominational backgrounds who are passionate about and committed to their way of worshiping. Conflict may occur. This can be an opportunity for your group to learn about and explore a variety of forms and styles of worship which are rooted in Scripture. For example, 1 Timothy 2:8 talks about praying with lifted and holy hands that represent pure lives. As small group worship develops, we learn from each other and expand our experiences of meeting with God.

Developing Group Worship

The worship life of a group will grow as members learn more about God and become more comfortable with each other. Below are some worship activities a leader might use at different steps in a group's worship development. These loosely correspond to the small group phases in chapter seven. Groups may take these steps at varying rates, beginning and ending in different places depending on the maturity and experience of the group members. Since groups may vary in size from four to fifteen people, what is done in worship may also vary. Some worship activities will naturally flow from the Scripture passage that's discussed.

Step 1: Checking Your Vision. In the early part of a group's life, especially if members are new Christians and new to each other, find out what worship experiences people have had. What are they comfortable with? Depending on what is discovered, the leader may not want to ask too much at this stage. For example, the leader could read a psalm, hymn or prayer and ask the group to reflect on God's character or pick out verses they particularly like. The group could also read a psalm together responsively. It might also be appropriate to play a recording of a worship song and discuss it together. For example, a worship song on Psalm 23 could be played when a group is discussing John 10 and Jesus as the good shepherd.

Step 2: Focusing Your Vision. Now the group might be ready for more creativity and participation. For example, a group could write a psalm of praise to God: The leader writes the first verse of a favorite psalm on the top of a piece of paper and each person composes a verse to write below, continuing on the same topic. At the end of a time of silence the leader reads the completed psalm. During this stage, the leader might also list different characteristics of God and ask the group which one meant the most to them during the past week. If the group is ready, this is a great time to begin singing together, possibly beginning with one or two brief and simple choruses.

Step 3: Expanding Your Vision. Once the group has bonded, members might be interested in trying some new things related to worship. Members could visit each other's churches. For example, seeing worship in another culture, language or denomination often shows us something new about God. The small group might also want to have a meeting in a local church or chapel. The group could spend time kneeling or raising hands in worship. Draw on the experiences of group members. Some groups have taken nature walks together and then spent some time praising God for his creation and character. This might also be a great time to read some devotional material together about God's character, like J. I. Packer's *Knowing God* (IVP).

Step 4: Deepening Your Vision. More mature groups might want to spend some extended time together around the theme of worship. For example, a group might spend a day together with some time in corporate worship, some time alone in personal worship and prayer, and then time together again to talk about what God has taught them about himself during that day. Extended times of singing, possibly with some prayers of praise and Scripture readings, often help people focus on God's nature.

As reflected in these steps, prayer is one of the most significant ways we experience worship in a small group. Since establishing and developing a small group's complete prayer life is one of the key responsibilities of a leader, the rest of the chapter will reflect that focus.

Praying Together on Campus

Amy became a Christian the summer before she started going to the small group Keisha led. Amy had never prayed much, while Keisha's African-American church always included lively times of corporate prayer. Keisha was looking forward to prayer being a part of small group. Some group members, like Amy, were new to prayer, while others had a variety of prayer experiences.

At one of the first meetings of the year, after taking a few prayer requests, Keisha enthusiastically invited anyone in the group to pray out loud, and she offered to close the prayer time. Amy sat in stunned silence as Rob said the Lord's Prayer. Judy prayed passionately and at length about every request, continually saying, "Father, we just . . . Father, we just . . ." Amy wondered how she could go on for so long without seeming to take a breath. Rick casually said, "Hey, God, thanks for helping me find my chemistry book." Keisha's closing prayer was so loud that Amy thought that God might have a bit of a hearing problem. At the end of the prayer time, Amy and a few others left the room so quickly that Keisha knew they felt uncomfortable.

After encouraging Amy to return to the group, Keisha reluctantly reverted to having one person open and close in prayer, knowing that this was a stop-gap measure until she could figure out how to meet the prayer needs of her group.

For many reasons prayer can be a struggle for small groups. It may be that some have never prayed out loud before. Other times it is because we are at different places in our prayer journey, are used to different prayer styles or are just uncomfortable because we are new to each other. Small group prayer time may also suffer because the leader doesn't have vision for this component.

As a result, some small groups never discuss their goals for prayer or their personal prayer struggles and experiences. The prayer time at the first meeting and the last meeting of the year may be identical; some members may never pray out loud or meet God in new ways. Prayer also can end up as an addendum as we are rushing out the door, making it more like a weak pulse than a group's heartbeat.

Praying Together in Acts

Moving back 2,000 years, we discover that when the early Christians prayed, it seems that often someone was praying out loud and others were listening, because Luke was able to record the prayers. Let's drop in on the prayer meeting in the early church described in Acts 4.

Peter and John have just been released from prison after being interrogated about healing a crippled man and preaching about Jesus. They also have been ordered by the Jewish authorities "not to speak or teach at all in the name of Jesus" (v. 18). Peter and John basically said they wouldn't be complying. When they joined their fellow believers and gave their report,

> They raised their voices together in prayer to God. "Sovereign Lord," they said, "you made the heaven and the earth and the sea, and everything in them. You spoke by the Holy Spirit through the mouth of your servant, our father David. . . .
>
> Indeed Herod and Pontius Pilate met together with the Gentiles and the people of Israel in this city to conspire against your holy servant Jesus, whom you anointed. They did what your power and will had decided beforehand should happen. Now, Lord, consider their threats and enable your servants to speak your word with all boldness. Stretch out your hand to heal and perform miraculous signs and wonders through the name of your holy servant Jesus."

After they prayed, the place where they were meeting was shaken. And they were all filled with the Holy Spirit and spoke the word of God boldly. (vv. 24-31)

John Stott in *The Message of Acts* quotes Walter Bauer on this passage, who notes that the praying together here "seems to go beyond mere assembly and activity to agreement about what they were praying for. They prayed 'with one mind or purpose or impulse.' " Fervent worship and prayer together is a significant part of church history.

Goals for Praying Together

Keisha's group did advance in prayer. This began when Keisha went to a small group leaders' meeting in which they talked about prayer goals and methods. Once she had some clear goals, she was better able to communicate with her group. Below are some common goals for prayer in InterVarsity small groups.

1. Over time, use different types of prayer in your meetings according to the leading of the Spirit and the openness of the group. The acronym *ACTS* is helpful in identifying the variety of prayers. *A*doration of God's nature is the worship part of prayer. Notice in Acts 4 how the early Christians began their prayer by praising God as the powerful King and Creator. *C*onfession of sins often happens in a worship service, but is part of our small group life as well. Groups can benefit from corporate prayers of repentance as well as audible and silent times of personal confession. *T*hanksgiving renews us as we are reminded of all the things God has done and all the prayers he has answered. There certainly is a spirit of thankfulness and there probably were prayers of thanksgiving at the Acts 4 prayer meeting. *S*upplication is talking to God about our own needs, the needs of group members and of the world. The early Christians were asking God for the boldness to continue their witness.

2. Use the Scripture under discussion as a springboard for the group prayer time. Notice how the early Christians in Acts 4 quoted Scripture in their prayer time. If Bible reading and discussion are God speaking to us, our prayer time should involve us responding to what God has said. For example, after studying Acts 4, it would be appropriate to pray about

barriers to evangelistic boldness, or if you are studying how John the Baptist called people to repentance, perhaps a silent time of confession should be the focus of the prayer time.

Sample Bible Discussion for Worship & Prayer Focus

1. What word would you use to describe your personal prayer life?
2. What keeps people from praying (in general)?
3. What keeps people from praying out loud or in groups?
4. What experiences have you had in group prayer?
5. Why should Christians pray together?
6. Why should Christians pray out loud?
7. What questions do you have about prayer?
8. Read Acts 4:23-31. How would you describe these believers?
9. How do they picture God?
10. What characterizes their prayer?
11. What can we learn from this prayer for our group's prayer life?
12. What goals or personal preferences do you have about group prayer? (Have everyone, including the leader, write down their answers, and then discuss your responses.)

Structure a prayer time that fits your group, possibly using activities from this chapter. You could pray sentence prayers, asking God to give you boldness to share your faith with one person. You could pray sentence prayers, asking the Sovereign Lord to enable some of your prayer goals to become reality.

3. Be attentive to different prayer preferences, styles, forms and experiences of people in the group who may come from different denominational and cultural backgrounds and try to accommodate them. For example, Rob's liturgical background might inspire him to bring a prayer from the Book of Common Prayer. Elizabeth might need people to say *Amen* or give some other verbal affirmation as she prays. Judy might occasionally like to have everyone pray out loud at once. Rick might want group members to touch him when they pray for him as was done in traditional Jewish blessings.

The leader's role here is crucial. It's important for the leader to acknowledge to the group that new prayer styles may be threatening and that these feelings are acceptable and normal. Encourage group members to bring these feelings before God and take some risks, which may then deepen their relationship with God. Talking about where different prayer forms originate in Scripture might be helpful as well.

4. Work toward incorporating conversational prayer in your small group. Conversational prayer involves the small group as a whole talking with God as if God were in the center of the circle. The conversation moves from topic to topic possibly with three or four people contributing on that topic as they listen to each other. Thus, conversational prayer consists of

☐ delineating some topics for prayer.

☐ praying for one topic at a time with a variety of people praying for aspects of that topic.

☐ often praying short prayers, possibly just adding a phrase to another's prayer. Individual prayers in this format often don't end "in Jesus' name." This phrase is used at the end of the whole "conversation," as the group is creating one long prayer together.

☐ speaking naturally to Jesus as if he were in the center of the circle.

This type of prayer has the advantage of a good conversation in that we are listening to each other and not quickly changing the subject or repeating what the other person has said. We also are listening to the Spirit prompting us to think of other angles for prayer on a topic. Because prayers are short, new people may pray, and we may be more attentive.

Steps for Praying Together

How did Keisha move the group toward growth in prayer? Like worship, the prayer life of a group evolves as members learn about prayer, learn from each other and grow more comfortable together. Although the leader has some goals for prayer life in mind, he or she also understands that it may take time to reach those goals. If the activities allow the spiritually new people to get involved in prayer early in the group's history, they'll be included as the group advances or tries new things. Bringing a group through the steps of prayer means knowing that groups take these steps at different rates and begin and end in different places.[1]

Step 1: Introduction. The leader may open and close in prayer. Doing this for a few weeks, while keeping the prayer time short and unthreatening, may be most helpful for everyone. Times of silent prayer and reflection may be appropriate here, as well as during other times of group life. Sometimes silent prayer is seen as elementary, but it can be significant, especially since our campuses often lack quiet. (See the *Small Group Idea Book* for a guided silent prayer exercise.) A group member may open or close the group in prayer, but ask ahead of time to avoid embarrassment in front of the group.

If a group includes people who aren't Christians, are inexperienced in prayer or are new to each other, they may need to spend some time in this step. If a group's purpose is evangelistic, there may be no prayer time. However, if seekers are coming to a group that has more than an investigative focus, some prayer is appropriate and probably expected. One doesn't need to be a Christian to address God.

Karen, who occasionally visited Keisha's group, said that being included in the prayer time, hearing others pray for her and praying herself were among the biggest things God used to bring her to faith.

Presenting prayer as something natural and easy is the best way for people to learn to pray. A one-to-one talk outside of small group or the prayer discussion described in step two provides an opportunity to express concerns and needs about prayer and be reassured.

Step 2: Prayer Discussion. After a few weeks or at an appropriate time, the leader may ask the group what their experiences have been in prayer, especially group prayer. This may also be a good time to talk about questions or frustrations with prayer. You could use the Bible study in the sidebar on page 78 to get people thinking about prayer. Then follow up by asking the group why Christians pray together and sometimes out loud. You may want to add some of the following insights.

Praying together brings unity and encouragement, increasing our faith. Praying together may have given the early Christians the courage in their Acts 4 prayer. When we hear others pray, we also learn about prayer. For example, Amy discovered new ways of praying by watching other group members—Rick's casualness in praying showed her that she could talk to God as a friend, and Elizabeth's habit of including Scripture when she prayed inspired Amy to do the same.

Praying out loud builds our relationships and community. For example, one night after discussing the passage in John 8 where a woman is caught in adultery, Keisha asked her group about ways they condemn people like the religious leaders condemned the woman in the passage. Amy told about some judgmental feelings toward her family. Hearing Rick, a young pray-er himself, bring her need before God encouraged and touched Amy and deepened her friendship with Rick as well.

Obviously, we want to beware of prayers designed to impress each other, and certainly there is always a time and place for private prayer. However, praying out loud gives us more incentive for personal prayer, which then brings enthusiasm for prayer back into the small group.

The leader should also talk about some prayer goals for the group. This entire discussion could take part or all of a small group time, possibly including a Bible discussion on Acts 4 or on one of the other prayers in Scripture, such as Nehemiah 1. The leader might then talk about taking steps, possibly small, to reach some of the leader's goals while integrating some of the ideas and experiences of the group members into future prayer times.

During the prayer discussion, Hae Won, Amy's friend, said that she couldn't imagine ever praying out loud. Keisha quickly reassured her that God hears silent prayers and that when she was ready, the group would welcome her verbal prayers as well.

Amy couldn't believe how much she learned about prayer in that one night. For example, she never knew why Christians prayed in Jesus' name. Now she knows how easy and important it is to talk to God in a group setting.

Keisha was also encouraged by what happened after the group discussion. Group members were honest, and some took risks in prayer. The group had agreed on some prayer goals, and Keisha knew that conversation with God would now be more central in her small group meetings.

Step 3: The Sound Barrier. The goal here, which may have been started with the prayer discussion, is to give the group a safe and simple way to begin praying aloud. One exercise that works well at this step is to give the group the introductory words to a sentence and ask individuals to complete the sentence in prayer randomly, one person at a time. Members can pray more than once. The sentence beginning could reflect the passage studied and might include: "Jesus, I thank you for . . ."; "Lord, I praise you for . . ."; and "Lord, I'm sorry for . . ." You might also begin with "Jesus you are . . ." and complete the sentence with different names of Jesus, like "the good shepherd," "the vine" and so on.

Another way to break the sound barrier is to ask everyone for a prayer request. Prayer then moves around the circle with each person praying for the person on the right. This may be challenging for some, but it does give members who are new to prayer some ideas of how to pray. At this step the group might also write prayer requests on cards and split into twos to pray at the meeting and/or during the week as prayer partners. Don't forget to talk about answers to prayer the following week.

Step 4: Modified Conversational Prayer. At this stage the leader is challenging the members to pray conversationally, while guiding them through the process. For example, the leader may read each petition of the Lord's prayer followed by a time for the group to respond to God as Father, and then to his holiness, our daily needs and so on.

Before Christmas, Keisha asked each member of the group to give a number of prayer requests. During prayer, Keisha introduced the name of each person and a number of people prayed through that person's requests.

Step 5: Conversational Prayer. The group is comfortable with praying out loud and listening to each other. Now they might be ready for some intensive prayer for one person who has a special need.

Rob's mother had been sick with cancer for a long time. One night, after asking Rob for his permission before the meeting, Keisha asked him to sit in the center of the group for special prayer for him and his family. First Keisha asked the group to be silent and to think about how Jesus might have them pray for Rob's family. Then the group, listening to God, each other and the Scriptures that God brought to mind, prayed conversationally for Rob, who was visibly moved and encouraged. Keisha could hardly believe this unified prayer was coming from the same people who had started praying together in September.

Some groups may have two prayer times, one where they may respond conversationally to the passage—possibly in praise, for friends who aren't believers or for a world concern—and a second focusing on personal needs.

Although it is a worthy one, conversational prayer may not be the goal of every group. Some people will never pray out loud in a group setting. Still, it is the leader's job to think carefully about the prayer time of the small group and to direct that time. The goal is to get the group thinking and talking about prayer and then doing it! Taking ideas from the group as well as using other creative prayer, worship and music ideas can make this a natural part of the meeting everyone looks forward to.

My sophomore year I had no space in my life for Dave, and, tragically, on some days there is little space in my life for a vision of God. This can happen in our small groups as well.

Keeping our small groups focused on God through worship and prayer, as the early Christians were in Acts 4, protects them from becoming academic discussions, one-sided conversations or social clubs. We are constantly reminding ourselves that God is present

Prayer Partners
by Cindy Meyers

Prayer partners are Christians who have committed themselves to an open and honest relationship. It is in some ways risky, but it is a risk that the Lord honors when two people become serious about meeting with him and growing together. As with any serious relationship, to build a prayer partnership costs time. Few prayer partners begin as David and Jonathan. Expect growth—and growing pains.

Prayer partners

☐ describe specifically what the Lord has taught them and what they know the Lord is trying to teach them.

☐ talk purposefully, avoiding a mere social session of aimless gabbing.

☐ pray specifically for one another's needs, for plans and for common concerns.

☐ pray purposefully, expecting God to act in their lives and willing to be used of God in answering their prayers.

☐ pray habitually, looking to the Lord as a first response to situations rather than as a last resort.

☐ pray for each other through the week and not just when together.

with us and desires our communication, our adoration and our obedience. He wants to teach us, hear us and refresh us for the week ahead. He may shake up our world. Very different people may learn to pray together. And people like Amy may learn how to pray and find that to be the most meaningful and encouraging part of their small group experience.

Understanding the Chapter
Study
1. Read Nehemiah 1. Describe Nehemiah and his prayer life.
2. What is Nehemiah's vision of God?
3. What types of prayer and worship are present here?

Reflect
1. Assess your vision of God. Where is your vision of God too small or distorted?
2. Where are you weak in your personal worship?
3. Where do you need to grow in your personal prayer life?
4. Think about the small group you were in last year. Whether or not your group had a worship time, how well did your group focus on the character of God?
5. Describe the prayer life of your last small group. (Was it participatory? How did it deepen? What did people learn about prayer?)

Apply
1. The strong personal prayer life of a leader will have an impact on the leader's small group. Set one goal today for your own prayer life.
2. Write a paragraph explaining why you think small group prayer together is important. Your enthusiasm will be the key.

---

[1]The prayer steps are adapted from Roger Gullick and Roberta Hestenes.

6/BECOMING WITNESSES: OUTREACH
■ Nina Thiel

We always wondered what God would do in a residence hall called *Trinity* at Cal Poly, San Luis Obispo. For years there had just barely been a Bible study there. Then one year, Sam and Lance moved in to lead a small group, and Bill and Eric moved in to back them up. They were determined to reach that mission field with the gospel.

Things started happening! A small group (of twenty!) formed around Sam and Lance, filled with new students who were eager to both grow in their faith and share it with others. People started coming to know Jesus. Nonbeliever's names were mentioned at the fellowship's daily prayer meeting. Everyone knew who to pray for in Trinity Hall.

In the winter, the small group sponsored an evangelistic talk. One of the new believers did all the publicity. The rest of the small group brought nearly 75 of their hallmates. After a two-hour question and answer time with the speaker, my husband, Larry, the small group members signed up over ten students for investigative Bible discussions that they would lead.

Since then small group members have recommitted themselves each year to living in Trinity and reaching Trinity with the gospel, and the tradition has continued. Trinity Hall is a place to meet Jesus. The list of students who have come to know him there is long.

Why should small groups see outreach as a significant component of their life together? The big reasons are Jesus' mandate: "Go and make disciples of all nations" (Matthew 28:19) and the fact that so many college students desperately need to know Jesus. InterVarsity exists to be a witness for Jesus on secular college and university campuses, to "glorify God by helping the entire campus to wrestle with the greatness of Christ" (*SGLH,* 1985, p. 21). The reason we locate our small groups in certain residence halls, apartment complexes, neighborhoods, academic departments, campus organizations, Greek houses or other student groupings should be to reach out together and bring those around us to Jesus.

God Calls Us to Reach Our World

From beginning to end, the Scripture itself is the story of God reaching to people, through people, to make them his children. When he called Abram apart in Genesis 12 to be the father of a new nation, belonging to God, he told him, "All peoples on earth will be blessed through you" (v. 3). When Jesus taught his disciples in the Sermon on the Mount, he told them they were the "salt of the earth" and the "light of the world," meant to be seen, in order that God would be praised (Matthew 5:13-16). In Jesus' final words to his disciples—after his resurrection, before his ascension—he tells his followers, "You will receive power when the Holy Spirit comes on you; and you will be my witnesses in Jerusalem, and in all Judea and Samaria, and to the ends of the earth" (Acts 1:8).

As I've worked with students, we have considered "Jerusalem" to be our campus community, "Judea and Samaria" to be the city which surrounds us, and the "ends of the earth" to be—the ends of the earth! We have committed ourselves to reaching out in evangelism, working for social justice and involving ourselves in the world mission of the church.

Those are noble intentions. The reality is many small groups never do a thing about the outreach component of their life together. Many leaders never plan outreach into their small group meetings, and if they do, it's usually the first thing to go. In some ways, outreach is the easiest element not to do. People come to a small group expecting to study the Bible, worship God, and to get to know, love and pray for each other. They do not always expect to be challenged to share their faith. Some of us find it easier to just not bring it up.

Ten Reasons a Small Group Must Take Outreach Seriously

1. A small group will grow closer by reaching out together. Some leaders worry that they have to build close relationships before even thinking about outreach. However, outreach is a great way to *build* close relationships. My husband, Larry, compares it to Little League All-Star teams. Kids from different teams, who would never even speak to each other, much less care about each other, when placed on an all-star team, are suddenly best friends. They are fighting a common enemy. They not only play their best, but cheer each other on. They are a real team. If your small group members are out all week, reclaiming territory from our Enemy, I guarantee that your times together will be much more precious and your relationships much deeper than if you merely focus on "feeling close."

2. A small group will die without outward focus. A group of people who only focus on each other becomes ingrown and unhealthy. They

Top Ten Reasons a Small Group Leader Shouldn't Plan for Outreach

10 If people start becoming Christians, we'll need a bigger room to meet in.

9 Praying for two friends to come to know Jesus isn't in my job description.

8 If everyone in my small group wants to go to India this summer, I'll have to go too.

7 Taking risks isn't good for my disposition.

6 If we become known as Christians in our dorm, people might start asking us questions about our faith.

5 Revival isn't in my one-year plan.

4 Serving the poor might make me uncomfortable with my lifestyle.

3 If our group stays small, everything will be under control.

2 Telling people about Jesus isn't politically correct.

1 Trusting God to use our small group to make a difference on campus, in the community and in the world is too much to ask.

will not grow closer without reaching out because they will not really need each other's encouragement. They will not know God better, because they won't be applying his Word in the world around them. When the year is over, the small group will end, leaving behind no trace of its existence.

A colleague of mine in Southern California compares groups that reach out together and groups that don't with a battleship and the Love Boat. Sailors on battleships keep in touch, have reunions, are in each other's weddings, name their children after each other, would lay down their lives for each other (and sometimes do). People cruising on the Love Boat might feel close for a time but their relationships are shallow. They never write; they don't remember each other's names; they are not a real family. If our small groups resemble love boats rather than battleships, they won't be real families either.

3. Small groups that reach out provide a model which members can take with them after graduation. Workplaces, neighborhoods, organizations, even churches will be changed as people with a mind for outreach enter, assuming "this is my mission field" and asking how they can reach it for Jesus. If your small group members learn to share their faith with their peers, learn to respond to the needs and issues in the cities surrounding their schools, and learn ways to be involved in worldwide mission, what an impact they will have as they continue to live out their faith after college!

4. A small group that sees itself as an outreach team will be great at helping its members discover and develop their spiritual gifts. When I asked Rob, a member of my small group at UNLV, to help me with an outreach table in the student union, I had no idea how gifted he was in outreach. He knew he was good at organizing, setting up information tables and making provocative displays, but he had never done it for Jesus. Others in my small group realized they were good at and enjoyed certain things about serving others. We all grew as we got out and reached out, doing things together to build the kingdom.

5. Any small group can learn to reach out. We don't wait until we're seminary professors to share our faith. Everyone can pray for their friends and prepare for opportunities to share Jesus with them. Everyone can

MILTON USES THE PERSONAL TOUCH TO BRING WITNESSING TO LIFE.

wipe off a table after a meal at a homeless shelter. Everyone can learn about a country that's been in the news lately to tell about in small group. Even the newest believer has a story to tell others; even the newest small group can get outreach into their DNA (as my writing colleague Doug is fond of saying). And if you have nonbelievers in your small group, don't panic! They'll probably love to serve in the community with you, as well as get involved in worldwide concerns. Once they understand why the Christians in your group want others to know Jesus, they might be happy to give the "non-Christian perspective" at an outreach event you plan together. Be sensitive (don't talk about needing to reach those poor pagan-heathens out there), but don't be shy or dishonest about what your hope would be for them and all their buddies—to meet Jesus and know his love for them.

6. A small group can provide the training and encouragement its members need to be faithful witnesses. Most things can be best accomplished on a small group level: Bible study, relationship-building, intercession—and encouragement in outreach. What a great place to pray for each others' nonbelieving friends, to learn how to share the gospel, to plan evangelistic experiences and service projects, to challenge each other to be bold, to encourage each other to be sensitive. Last spring my small group did the "30 Day Plan" together (see *Small Group Idea Book*). The program challenged us to work at really natural activities we should all be doing anyway, like praying daily for opportunities to share Jesus, meeting people, doing things with nonbelieving friends, inviting them to Christian things and asking what they think about Jesus. Everyone was good at some aspects and weak at others. We had some great discussion time about where we were weak evangelistically and how we could grow in those areas, and some great times of prayer for each other.

7. *A small group can be easily organized within a specific "people group."* If you have two leaders ready to roll in a certain residence hall, department, sorority or athletic team, you can reach everyone else in that people group with the gospel by designing opportunities for all of them to have the chance to meet Jesus. Placing small groups strategically like this makes reaching the whole campus with the gospel a more realistic goal. You could put each small group on a map to see where the holes are in the fellowship's witness—and to see when you've got the campus covered.

Back to Sam, Lance, Bill and Eric in Trinity Hall. They picked that residence hall to move into and minister in because no other leaders from the fellowship were planning to live there. Their approach and timing were great!

8. *A small group is a visible, accessible representative of Jesus—more accurate than one lone evangelist.* As we work hard at growing close to Jesus and to each other, and as we work together to reach out around us, nonbelievers get the chance to see the body of Christ at work. What an attractive alternative to the empty relationships and pursuits all around us! The earliest church enjoyed "the favor of all the people," and "the Lord added to their number daily those who were being saved" (Acts 2:47).

At a goodby party for a graduated-and-leaving member of Larry's small group, a nonbelieving friend who was included in the party commented to me: "These people seem to really love each other. These are good relationships." I'm not sure she realized it, but what this friend saw was Jesus at work in a small group of his people.

9. A small group can provide the perfect opportunity for nonbelievers to "come and see" (John 1:46). Surrounded by friends in a casual environment, the Scriptures are opened and discussed. Friends can ask questions and get answers. They can be prayed for. They can see Jesus for themselves. Small groups that are good at reaching out are also good at including others without getting freaked out or being anything but natural.

Benton began attending a small group, at the invitation of one of its members, before he decided to follow Jesus. They studied Jesus in John's Gospel, and before long Benton joined the discussion as a believer, eager to know Jesus better so that he might follow him more closely.

10. Without Jesus people are lost, and with Jesus they're made alive (Luke 15)! God has given us the awesome privilege of building the kingdom by bringing others to Jesus wherever we are. This is true for us individually; it is also true for our small groups.

Benton was actually one of two people who came to know Jesus in the same small group. Michelle had been invited by a different small group member. Looking back, both of them say they now know they were lost before they met Jesus because they didn't know then that they were lost. Benton came from a sporadic religious background (including Mormonism) which had no effect on the way he lived. Michelle came from a more consistent church background in which "faith was personal," meaning you believe something in your head and no one will ever know the difference.

Benton knew he was different from the Christians in the small group—he noticed their excitement, their zeal for life and for Jesus. Michelle dressed up the first time she came to the small group because she didn't realize how casual it would be. Both Michelle and Benton say that it was seeing Jesus for themselves in the Scriptures—what he said, who he was, what he did for them and what it meant to follow him—that convinced them both to give their lives to him (by December).

Benton felt the presence of God and the peace of God, and knew he would never have to worry again, because (in his words) "God knows me and I know God." And though obedience wasn't always easy, he never doubted or resisted; he knew that what Jesus said, he should do. Michelle's new life grew in intensity when the small group went on a one week mission to a local ministry in a village in Mexico. Sharing her testimony for the first time, praying with her partners-in-ministry and studying Jonah together helped develop her zeal to tell others about Christ too.

When I asked them what difference the small group made in their decision to follow Jesus, Michelle said that it was being encouraged to say what she thought during small group that made her feel comfortable. Benton remembers how patient everyone was with him and how they never treated him differently or like an outsider; he was included in everything. He especially remembers the time the small group took to pray for him and praise God when he decided to follow Jesus.

Reaching Your Jerusalem

Use your small group meetings to prepare your members for doing evangelism on campus. You might read and discuss the IVP booklet *Pizza Parlor Evangelism* by Rebecca Manley Pippert. Then fill out a 2+ card (available in *Small Group Idea Book*), each praying for at least two nonbelieving friends together and taking some risk in those relationships, in the following week, to bring them closer to Jesus. Or you might prepare by doing some studies on how Jesus related to different kinds of nonbelievers, and then throwing a party in your living area just as a way of having fun with and getting to know those who live around you. Preparation could include studying the Gospels together, as well as getting some training in how to lead an investigative Bible discussion (IBD). Doing could include having members of the small group host a four-week IBD for their friends. Or work through an outline of the gospel, memorizing some of the verses and role-playing with each other. The following week ask a friend what he thinks about Jesus or if she knows what Christians really believe. Preparation could include researching answers to often-voiced objections to Christianity. Doing could include asking friends what their questions are and attempting to answer them.

Most university programs work with a "wellness" model, which includes spiritual wellness. A small group or two in each residence hall can
go to the hall government or coordinators with great options for programming in that realm. To pull off a successful event, group members need
to prepare well in advance, getting permission to use the biggest lounge
in the hall, inviting a well-qualified speaker or arranging to use a good
video, doing publicity beforehand and having a plan for discussion afterward. Members need to be ready to invite and bring their hallmates. They
need to be ready to follow up the evening with conversations about the
gospel deep into the night. They need to plan to bring new people into
their small group, or to plan special investigative Bible discussions for
several weeks following.

On commuter campuses, or for something smaller scale on residential
campuses, small groups can plan special evenings when everybody brings
their seeking friends for a special Bible study/discussion or video-and-
discussion, then all go out for frozen yogurt afterward. It could turn into
a weekly event. If small groups are arranged by academic departments,
apartment complexes or affiliation with certain campus organizations,
they could plan special outreach events for those "people groups" accordingly. Get Christian professors and professionals involved in helping you
reach students.

Small groups can also get involved in outreach through service projects
and justice issues on campus. I have heard of small groups lobbying for
the building of wheelchair-accessible entrances to older buildings on campus or protesting the racist and sexist hiring practices of their universities.
A small group could participate in special activities during Black History
Month or Women's History Month to learn from, support and befriend
those in traditionally oppressive situations on campus. At one campus, a
small group essentially became the international student services office
because so little was being done to help students from overseas. Your
campus might not resemble UC—Berkeley in the 1960s, but on most
campuses, the opportunities for speaking up—and doing something—in
the name of Jesus regarding social issues are plentiful.

One great way to get involved in evangelism on campus is to tie into "whole chapter" evangelistic events. Your small group could take a day at the outreach table outside the student union. You can talk and pray about who each of you will bring to hear an open-air evangelist, dramatic presentation, media event or some other special speaker. You can all go together to a whole-chapter evangelism workshop or conference.

I'll never forget the faithfulness and enthusiasm of the five small groups in Sierra Madre Hall when the fellowship brought a large multimedia production to Cal Poly for three big showings. Before each one, all the small group leaders, almost all the small group members and a whole gang of people from their halls arrived to see the show. Those small groups did a great job of using an all-chapter event to help them reach out together.

Week-to-week ask what's happening in the area of evangelism for your group: Who can we be praying for? Who have you been hanging out with? Who have you been sharing with? What can our group do to help? This can make a big difference in members' attitudes about being "salt and light" on their campus. Evangelism becomes who we are instead of what we do. Reaching out to others becomes a foundational value of small group life.

Reaching Your Judea and Samaria

Many of our most prestigious, upscale universities are surrounded by areas of incredible poverty and racial tension. The University of Southern California, on the edge of south-central Los Angeles, is a prime example of this. During the Los Angeles riots in the spring of 1992, the InterVarsity Fellowship at USC was having their regular large-group meeting, a bit unaware of the situation that was brewing right off campus. By the end of their meeting, the word had come from resident advisors that everyone needed to return to their dorms and not leave the campus (beefed-up campus security guarded the gates of the school). So the InterVarsity staff and others from off-campus spent the night on campus, hardly sleeping, mostly praying together and watching the news.

The next day, as the L.A.P.D. made the dorm cafeteria one of their headquarters, the InterVarsity fellowship met to decide how to respond to the rioting. Many left the campus and L.A. (by order of their parents).

But many decided to stay as an expression of their membership in and commitment to the rapidly disintegrating community surrounding their campus. That night, those who stayed met to pray and make plans. The next day, those staff and students joined a few brave others (since the police still didn't have the situation under control) to begin the clean-up process. The day after that, they were joined by teams of InterVarsity staff and students from other L.A. area schools. They had found a very relevant way to reach their community with Christ's love.

Almost every city has a homeless population, forgotten elderly people and neglected children. We can prepare our members to deal with these areas of incredible need by learning about them, inviting experts in to teach us, studying the Scriptures to see how God feels about the poor and the abandoned. We can minister in the communities around our campuses by hooking up with a ministry to the homeless or bringing songs and conversation into a nursing home.

The InterVarsity group at Bakersfield College, a community college in California, started an after-school athletic program for children who would otherwise have nowhere else to go. Students from Occidental College in the Highland Park area east of Los Angeles spend their afternoons as tutors for inner-city children at a local church. Many campuses these days are tapping into students' willingness to serve in the cities around them. Your whole small group could get involved in a "big sister/big brother" program or go together on a campus-planned "alternative spring break" to serve in some area of great need in the community (and you don't have to plan it!). There are also summer opportunities for a whole small group to participate together in, or even send just a couple of your members to an InterVarsity urban project.

Before you get overwhelmed with all these ideas, let me encourage you with little ways a small group can care for people in the community. Many small groups at UNLV went once to help serve dinner at the Salvation Army in downtown Las Vegas; we were changed (and educated), and people were fed. Clothing and canned food drives are easy to arrange and very helpful to homeless shelters. Prayer for the city is simple to organize but incredibly important to God's work and his people who minister there every day. Once we get in the habit of caring for the world around our little world (on campus, at work or at home), our small groups will graduate people who God will continue to use to reach Judea and Samaria.

Reaching the Ends of the Earth

In my life the paradigm of "learning, praying, sending and going" has been helpful as a framework for my own involvement in world missions. It works well for small groups too. I've even had groups brainstorm ideas for each and choose together what our group will do to love the world for Jesus.

To help your small group learn about the world and missions, you could do some Bible studies on God's care and plan for all the nations of the world. Start in Genesis and end in Revelation. It's all there. A good microcosm is in the book of Acts. You could also read a book about missions or some missionary biographies together. Start a current events time in your group when people come prepared to share what's going on internationally that week. Give research assignments to learn more about countries in the news. As a group, pick a continent, country or people group to adopt for the year (or beyond) to learn about and pray for; *Operation World,* compiled by Patrick Johnstone, is a key resource. Together, sponsor a child through Compassion International or World Vision; learn about her country; pray for her needs; meet some financial needs. As a group, you could befriend some international students, offer help with English and classwork, learn all about their home countries and have a great influence overseas for Jesus without ever even leaving campus. Participate as a group in the international student club or the events of other ethnic-specific organizations on campus. Participate in campus-sponsored fasts for world hunger relief, or sponsor one yourselves. Plan to go as a group to Urbana, InterVarsity's triennial student mission convention, during Christmas break.

To help your small group pray for the world, you could set aside time to pray for all the things you're learning about—current events, specific countries, international students and sponsored children. Pray for each other and the plans you've all made as a result of Urbana or your reading and study of world missions. Many InterVarsity groups are connected with specific missionaries or staff of International Fellowship of Evangelical Students in other countries; your small group could pledge to pray for them. If your fellowship's chapter prayer meeting has a worldwide component to it, go as a group to pray. If it doesn't, your group could volunteer to start and lead a world-concerns prayer meeting for the chapter. It's likely that members of your group know actual missionaries or ministries overseas (especially if they're from there) that the whole group could embrace in prayer.

Once you've learned and prayed, put on the fundraising cap and meet some physical needs. This includes raising money for any of the ministries you've prayed for—relief organizations, sponsorship programs, student workers overseas or specific missionaries. A lot of InterVarsity chapters regularly send out summer missionaries; if one is in your group, your group has the incredible opportunity to "get behind" that brother or sister and get them the money they need to get overseas. If one isn't in your group, adopt one. One way to raise money is through the giving of group members; the other is to do a mongo fundraiser together. Both approaches are challenging and good for small group members and the mission they're supporting.

Finally, a small group can live out a concern for the world by going overseas or into another culture. This could be as big as going together on an InterVarsity global project for most of the summer, or as small as a vacation week spent serving people in a nearby foreign country (admittedly easier for those living in the Southwest). My colleague, Shawn Young, took his whole small group from the frosh residence hall at UNLV (including one or two nonbelievers) to Mexico with others from the fellowship for a five-day service project with a local mission near Encinada. One year, students from Cal Poly—San Luis Obispo organized a one-week trip to a mission on a Native American reservation in Arizona. A whole small group could even spend a semester overseas on an exchange program through the college. You could all end up together somewhere permanently!

Putting It All Together

My colleague at USC, Kevin Blue, told me a great story that integrates everything this chapter is about. A senior in a summer Bible study met an international student from Japan and invited him to join the fellowship as they made and served dinner in MacArthur Park and talked to people about the gospel. The non-Christian Japanese student went along to the park—a place of poverty and drug-dealing with a large African-American homeless population. This young man was shocked at what he saw. He had never seen poor people before, and he was amazed to see the students, obviously not poor people, crossing economic and racial lines to serve others. He was really stirred, and after the summer left for Japan with great curiosity and determination to study the Bible. He expressed his gratefulness for the experience of serving with the Christians in the park, by leaving a special "you're family now" gift from his home village with the student who had invited him. Kevin doesn't know if the student from Japan had become a Christian, but he did know that the American student who met him is still in touch. Campus, community and world were impacted in one experience!

There are so many things a small group can do to reach out together. Our campuses, communities and world are certainly needy places filled with people who would respond eagerly to the love of Jesus shown through his people, whether in conversation or in acts of mercy and servanthood. Our groups will draw close to God and to each other as we take risks together to reach out. Even a goal of doing one or two "activities" in each area—Jerusalem, Judea and Samaria, and the ends of the earth—each quarter or semester can make a big difference in the growth of members in their commitment to evangelism and service and in the numeric growth of the kingdom of God. That's an opportunity we don't want to miss!

Understanding the Chapter
Study

1. Read Acts 1:1-11. List all the ways Jesus "passes the baton" to his followers.

2. What is involved in becoming witnesses for this group hidden away in Jerusalem? (See it going down in Acts 2!)

Reflect

1. Looking at the top ten list of reasons to do outreach (and the sidebar of reasons not to), why should a small group plan to be involved in outreach?

2. Why is outreach sometimes harder to do than the other components of small group life?

3. Give an example of when you've seen outreach to be worth the effort.

4. Think about your current small group and the overall small group ministry on your campus. How are you doing at reaching out?

5. Are your efforts well distributed between outreach on campus, involvement in the community and concern for the world, or are they lopsided? Explain.

Apply

1. Brainstorm ideas for reaching each area of Acts 1:1-11—Jerusalem, Judea and Samaria, the ends of the earth—for your unique campus and small group situation. If you're a small group leader, do this with your small group after a study of Acts 1:1-11.

2. Write down one idea for outreach in each area that you could do in your small group's very first time together.

PART 3
NAVIGATING GROUP LIFE

7/Guiding Through Phases

8/Cultivating Group Ownership

9/Encouraging Good Communication

10/Redeeming Conflict

Taken from *Faith in Orbit* © 1995 by Mary Chambers and used by permission of InterVarsity Press.

"YOU KNOW, MOST BIBLICAL SCHOLARS NOW AGREE THAT THE WHOLE QUESTION OF RIGHT AND WRONG WAS A CULTURAL THING."

7/GUIDING THROUGH PHASES
■ Sara Keiper

September 5: *Tonight is my first meeting. Attending small group leaders camp, praying all summer and coming back to campus a week early has been good preparation. But suddenly I don't feel ready. I'm scared; I'm excited. Lord, please help me tonight. Help me to love the people you bring. Make all of us fall more in love with you, become true friends and be a witness on campus.*

God has chosen to give us some of his richest blessings through loving and committed relationships. I doubt there is any gift more precious than true friendship. Friendship makes discipleship more enjoyable, and discipleship makes friendship more significant. One of the ways God forms and shapes us and accomplishes his purposes is through our life together.

Small groups are made up of people who are different from each other. Members bring their hopes, dreams, fears and past experiences (the good ones and the not-so-good ones). We also bring our own ethnic distinctives and God-given personalities. So as the small group leader, how in the world can you bring these diverse individuals together in active, caring community? This is the question that Jim, a new small group leader, faced as he wrote the journal entry above. Traveling through a year with Jim will help us prepare for our own journeys.

The Process of Friendship

Think about your most treasured friends. I would guess that there was a process from the time you first met to the time when you called that person *friend*. Remember the initial enjoyment, the eagerness to be together more, the discovery of common interests? C. S. Lewis explains it this way: "Friendship is born at the moment when one says to another, 'What, you too? I thought no one but myself . . .' " *(The Four Loves).*

Then comes the time in most relationships, sigh, when there is a disagreement or misunderstanding or important areas of differences are discovered. This can feel very disappointing or even frightening. But it is precisely during these hard times that significant roots of trust and commitment can be put down. If we are willing to allow one another to be who we are, not fleeing when a difficult area is revealed, a wonderful thing can happen. We begin becoming authentic friends.

This same journey can be taken by a group. Knowing about the process of growth in group life will give you guidelines to help you recognize, anticipate and even assist your group in their journey. Take care to remember that these are only *guidelines.* The process will vary some because you, the group, and God's desires for you are all unique factors. You may do all the right things, all the things you know to do, and still folks will drop out or be dissatisfied. The important thing is being faithful to what God has called you to, trusting him for what he wants to accomplish.

The Four Phases

Groups grow through four somewhat predictable phases that have some common characteristics and similar challenges. They are *start-up, shake-up, live-it-up* and *wrap-up.* Understanding what people are thinking and feeling during each phase can help you guide your group through the journey. As a leader, understanding your own thoughts and feelings will give you helpful insights as you navigate the process. As you pass through each phase, you lay the foundation for the next phase.

All groups go through these phases in one way or another. They may not make it through all of them or may move back and forth between them. The group of your dreams would experience all four phases in a logical, timely manner. But just like the man or woman of your dreams, groups aren't perfect. Most groups move one step forward, then may seem to take two steps backwards and some seem to get stuck forever in a particular phase. Sometimes there seems to be no reason for this (only God knows), but often there are ways to nudge the group along. Knowing what people are likely to be thinking and feeling along the way will enable you to address needs that may remain unspoken. This kind of caring will help you to move through the phases.

Start-Up

Ruth Ann was a freshman. Her older sister's one piece of advice to her was "find a campus fellowship that has small groups as soon as you get to campus." So Ruth Ann stopped by several information tables on registration day, leaving her name and interest in joining a small group. Within a few days, she got a call from one fellowship. They told her they only wanted people with a "high degree of commitment." Ruth Ann thought, "How can I make a commitment to a group of people I've never met and a leader I know nothing about? I don't even know what I'm being asked to commit to."

Then a knock came at her door. It was Jeff and Susan inviting her to come to their small group the next night. "Come and meet everyone else and get to know us," they said. "We'll tell you more about what we have planned and what we're going to study, and we'd also like to hear what you'd like." Ruth Ann felt a surge of hope, interest and even excitement as she anticipated going to the group.

We initially come to small groups with some degree of desire for relationships. We also bring a range of ambivalent feelings, from high hopes to nagging doubts: Who are these people? Will they accept the real me? Will I be able to trust the leader? What are the purposes of the group? All these questions are an *exploration* of what the group is about and the potential for finding a place of belonging.

The questions and feelings of start-up are seen in excessively polite conversation on "safe" topics. Conversation is about where you're from, what dorm you live in, your major, where you get your hair cut and so on—facts that don't require a strong personal opinion.

Some will look for common areas of interest, avoiding areas of discomfort or pushing aside potential "personality clashes." These folks are highly motivated to see the group come together. They are committed to the group from the moment it takes off. Others are more cautious, needing more time to trust others before they can let people really know them. Differences and potential conflicts raise questions about whether this is the group for them.

Group members want two things as the group begins. There is a longing to be able to trust others, to be known, to be real, and to feel liked and trusted. And at the same time conflict is feared and usually avoided. There is internal tension between the desire to belong and the fear of being hurt and disappointed.

All these thoughts, feelings and questions need to be addressed. In your first three to four meetings communicate, *each time,* information about the group—when, where and what. Talk about purposes and expectations. Let them in on your dreams for them individually and as a growing group of friends. Being open about yourself will be an example.

Welcome people wherever they are, both those with a personal relationship with Jesus and those who want to find out more about Jesus. State common factors that have brought you all together, but also acknowledge differences and diversity as good things that God can use for spiritual growth. Saying these things will ally some unspoken fears and build trust in your leadership.

Give directions and information that show that you prayed for them even before you knew them and that you spent time and energy planning. Remind them of God's love and involvement in their lives individually and together.

Leaders need to take lots of initiative with people in start-up. Call, meet for ice cream, a walk or Frisbee throwing to find out more about who folks are, where God is at work in them and what they would like to see happen in the group. Talk again of your hopes and dreams and let them see God in your life too. If the group is large, it will be hard to meet with everyone. You may want to meet with folks in pairs.

The Leader's Needs

This is a time of hopeful anticipation. You will expend a lot of time and energy. Let your prayer support team (get one if you don't have one) know how things are going. Don't neglect your own time with God, and make it a priority to meet with other small group leaders as well.

Having a co-leader helps share the time and energy.

How your early meetings are handled will influence whether the cautious folks will hang in there. Some may decide that this isn't the group for them. That's okay. People are exploring in start-up.

In order to have a good middle and a good end you need a good beginning. Just because the start-up phase is the beginning does not mean that it is unimportant and should be hurried through or jumped over in order to get to the "real thing." It *is* the real thing!

Shake-Up

Let's sneak a peak into Jim's log again: *What is going on with this group? Everything seemed to be going along so well. But these last two weeks strangers have shown up. Grumpy, irritable, impatient people. I'm tired of Steve's phone messages saying that I should make Nancy stop talking so much. Good grief, he's the one who talks too much. I wonder why Celia has stopped coming, and Justin is always late. Maybe I don't have what it takes to be a small group leader. I wish I hadn't agreed to do this. This is not what I signed up for. Lord, give me wisdom and love.*

As the superficial relationships of the start-up phase become less satisfying, the desire for deeper friendship and more activity grow stronger. Trust is growing and people are becoming more open and honest. The group has experienced enjoyable times of Bible study, prayer and fun. They have also been together long enough to see or discover areas of diversity that may be irritating or hard to understand and difficult to accept. Learning to be true friends means learning to love, pray, encour-

Taken from *Reborn to Be Wild* ● 1993 by Doug Hall and used by permission of InterVarsity Press.

It's the night of the County Mildew Festival, and Gene's study of 2 Chronicles fails to weather the competition.

age and care, to hang in there rather than fleeing when struggles come or an unattractive side surfaces.

Some folks in the group become discouraged, attending sporadically or not at all. Caring for them at this point means asking what is troubling them—but be ready to have your leadership criticized. At the same time the group is ready to be asked for a greater commitment if it is to move forward on the journey toward a community of friends. This community is not perfect. These people are not perfect. The group has found its way into a time of *transition* called *shake-up.*

Some groups navigate this phase smoothly; others will find it rocky or even turbulent. This can be an emotional time for the group. The group is facing the diversity that God delights in. God wants to give new, deeper experiences with these new friends we might not have chosen on our own.

Questions people will have during shake-up have to do with ownership and deeper trust: Why is this person the leader? How are decisions made? Can I influence decisions? Can I be more honest? Do I want to make a bigger commitment to the group? (Chapter eight will delve deeper into the ownership question.)

Shake-up can be a difficult phase for leaders. The group is testing your trustworthiness as well as their own level of commitment. Try to avoid being defensive. Confronting will confirm fears about being more open and diminish their sense of worth in the group. Treating critical people with love and respect, sincerely seeking to understand them, will go a long way in deepening trust and developing greater commitment. For some this may be the first experience when conflict is dealt with in a caring, respectful manner. Believe that God is at work even when the weirdness sets in. Continue to model an open, honest, hopeful, encouraging attitude.

Some of the challenges that surface during shake-up can be dealt with in the group, and some may be more wisely handled one-on-one. Read chapter ten on redeeming conflict. Talk the situation over with your small group coordinator. Ask for help at your small group leaders' meetings or tell a trusted friend who is praying for you. This is no time to be a lone ranger.

When Paul joined the small group I was leading, things changed. Although committed to the group, Paul frequently seemed frustrated with Lynn, Gary and Sue, who were younger Christians. He kept trying to move the discussions to a higher theological level than the group was ready for. Sue and Lynn began to come late and leave immediately after the meeting, and Gary stopped his fledgling attempts to pray out loud. We were on a crash-and-burn course. I had to do something.

The easy solution seemed to be to tell Paul that he didn't fit; another group might be more satisfying. As I prayed, however, that didn't seem to be God's solution. Instead, one morning I got bagels and met with Paul for breakfast. I expressed my appreciation for his commitment to the group and the Bible knowledge that he brought. Then I asked him how he thought the group was doing.

Paul immediately began blaming Gary for what he saw as superficial discussions. As I asked questions, trying to understand better, Paul became less angry, still grumpy, but more able to listen as well as talk. Although it felt risky, I pointed out how his impatience affected the others. Paul was shocked. He hadn't meant to hurt anyone. He genuinely liked the people in the group. I gently challenged Paul: while this group might not have the most stimulating Bible study from his perspective, perhaps God wanted to teach him something different. Paul could contribute greatly to Lynn, Sue and Gary's spiritual growth if he developed friendships with them. We prayed together that Paul would be more open to what God had for him in this small group.

The next time our group met, much to my surprise, Paul asked the group to forgive him for his impatience and told them how glad he was to be with them. Gary prayed a wonderful prayer of appreciation for Paul that evening, and friendships were deepened. I quietly cheered, thanking God for the privilege of watching him at work.

Meeting with folks outside of the group meeting is helpful. You can talk with people about attitudes or relationship problems you have noticed. When this is done in a loving way, it can be received as a sign of caring friendship. You might also invite two members to have coffee with you. This will help build their relationship as well. Continue to love and pray for your group; this is the most important thing you can do.

Some groups get stuck here. Some or all of the members may be afraid or unable to be known more deeply or take more risks. Perhaps the leader doesn't know how to or is afraid to bring up whatever it is that is inhibiting group growth and thinks it's easier to stay in a more familiar place. Other groups may be content, not feeling the need to grow beyond this point. Shake-up can be emotionally charged or emotionally flat, draining or energizing. As the leader, you will definitely know when you are in it and you will definitely cheer when you are through it if shake-up has been a tense time for your group.

Not all groups have a rocky journey in shake-up. I had been meeting with a group of nursing students for three months. They had many classes and clinical labs together, seemed to like each other, enjoyed Bible study and worship, and came faithfully. Yet something was missing. There didn't seem to be evidence of growing depth in their friendship. They had a "nice" time together, but no spark.

One evening I changed the usual format and spent the entire meeting on an exercise called the *shield*. (See *Small Group Idea Book*.) People answered some important questions about themselves depicted in words or pictures in different places on the shield: Who influenced you the most?

Where do you feel most at home? What is your greatest accomplishment? What three words would you like said about you? An amazing thing happened. They discovered hopes, dreams, fears, disappointments, hurting moments—deeper places where God was at work. Things that hadn't been told before.

When the group prayed that night there was a new depth of knowing, caring and trusting that lasted and even grew throughout the year. To pray more they set up "prayer triplets," groups of three who met to pray together according to class schedule. At the end of that meeting I realized that, without any manipulation on my part, God had moved us through the shake-up phase and on to live-it-up.

Live-It-Up

November 20: God gave me so much to be thankful for this Thanksgiving.

Our group survived shake-up. And I survived. Yippee! Praise God! My small group coordinator's wise advice on dealing with conflict really helped. We're not perfect, but I noticed people making plans for lunch. Kevin and David rallied the group to help Marcia move. Joe offered to make the flyer for next semester. Many are so full of ideas all of a sudden, making plans without even asking me at times. I actually feel a bit left out. Thank you, Lord, for moving us to deeper friendship and community. Help me to understand my mixed feelings.

You know your group has

The Leader's Needs

This can be a lonely and frustrating time if your group has an intense journey through shake-up. You may feel like renaming it *blow-up* or *give-up* or even *throw-up*, if you are a nursing or pre-med student. But cheer-up! The good things that God gives and does in shake-up can bring depth, quality and maturity. Remember too that only the Holy Spirit can change hearts. You are there to help create an atmosphere where he can work.

Don't take things too personally; this is a normal phase. Problem solve with others. Make it a priority to be meeting and praying with other leaders, so you can benefit from their experience, encouragement and prayers. Let your prayer support team know how you are doing, not just what's happening in the group.

made the journey to the next phase, live-it-up, when the group shows a sense of security in their friendships and a growing excitement about doing things together. Diversity enriches and energizes, and conflict becomes an opportunity for growth. Folks are learning to serve each other, finding practical ways to care outside the meetings. The group experiences joy in God's work among them. There will always be diversity, and understanding each other requires work, but loyalty and commitment is demonstrated and each person feels valued and accepted. Gifts emerge and are offered to benefit each other. Life is fuller and more complete in this community of true friends. This is a lively time of dealing with real issues in a caring way.

In this phase there is a mutual willingness to commit to some activity. People are asking: How can *we* meet *our* goals? First, what can *we* commit *our*selves to? Second, what is my part? How the group moves forward will vary widely. Each group will seek and find its own character and ministry. There is no witness more powerful to those around you than the loving friendships that Jesus has created among believers.

Even though the group members are taking more ownership, the leader has an important contribution in live-it-up. As the group gets excited about doing more together, you can help the group to evaluate the many possibilities in light of what God has given them to work toward. As you meet with folks outside the meetings, help them discover and develop their gifts so they can contribute to the life of the group. You may be seen as less active "up front" now, but you are very active as you pray, develop people and keep God's goals before them.

Judy had led her group through start-up, shake-up and into live-it-up. She had poured herself into these women, loving them and challenging them on their journey as individuals and friends. When they hit live-it-up, some in the group were eager to develop and use their gifts in the group. Judy spent a lot of time teaching Katie to prepare and lead Bible studies. Katie took to it like a duck to water, becoming a gifted Bible study leader, even better than Judy. Judy was delighted to see someone she loved grow in skill. And with Katie leading the Bible study Judy had more time available to help others in the group develop their gifts.

In this phase groups often want to respond more actively to Scripture. A small group of nursing students at Merritt College were studying parables and thinking about what it meant to be a neighbor. They prayed for God to show them ways to demonstrate Jesus' love in their dorm. An idea began to form that excited even the most timid. They would hold a "Recovery Room" in the lounge during exam week. Back rubs, neck rubs, snacks (made by alumni), short games and even prayer would be available. Recent graduates would help the students carry out their plan.

"Recovery Room" was a roaring success and even became a yearly tradition. Comments like "No one has ever cared for us this way" came from the students, dorm staff and even the dean. People responded with appreciation and a new openness to InterVarsity, Nurses Christian Fellowship and, most importantly, Jesus.

Wrap-Up

April 30: This year has flown by. So much has happened. I'm relieved it's over, but at the same time I don't want it to end. Lord, you have been so faithful to me, keeping me from giving up, providing wisdom and giving me joy, even when we had that rough stretch. Help me plan our next few meetings together so we can remember how good you have been.

As long as we live on this earth, relationships will experience times of separation and ending. Most of us don't know how to say goodby very well—or very easily. Time pressure and low energy can sometimes cheat us out of experiencing a meaningful conclusion. However, if wrap-up is not planned for, there can be a sense of incompleteness. The group will also miss out on the joy of remembering and celebrating what God has done in their community of friends. Rough spots can be celebrated

The Leader's Needs

As the group assumes a sense of energy and enthusiasm that is not as dependent on the leader, you may feel left out, left behind or even unappreciated. This means you are doing a good job. Your work is to continue to love the group, pray for them and with them, encourage them on their journey and be pleased that you have been a part of God's work.

because God is at work. Even if your group didn't navigate all the phases and whether your group will meet again after the semester break or will never be together again until heaven, don't skip over this phase. In fact, you really should be planning for wrap-up when you start-up.

The ending of a year, a group or a study series will mean something different to each person. It can be a time of great joy and exhilaration. This is also a time to discover and express areas of disappointment. There may also be some unfinished business between people. It can be painful and sad, as well as a celebration all at the same time. For some it may be a relief. Others may approach wrap-up more matter-of-factly. The range of feelings and thoughts and questions is wide. Group members think: Was it worth it? What have I learned? How have I changed? What did God teach me in the study, through these friends of mine? What have I learned about God? others? myself?

The three parts of wrap-up are *evaluation, appreciation* and *celebration.* During *evaluation* we look at what worked and what didn't. How was the meeting time and place and topic of study? What was most beneficial? What could have been left out or done differently? The leader invites and welcomes honest, helpful comments, even ones that are lovingly critical. (*Small Group Idea Book* has a sample evaluation form.) Giving people time to think though these questions and jot down some thoughts before discussion with the whole group will generate more thoughtful information. Whatever is said during the discussion, leaders should take care to thank people for their honesty and contribution.

Appreciation involves telling or showing what you are grateful to the group for. One way to do this is to have each person take a turn being "it." The others then say how they have appreciated and been influenced by that person. We seldom take time to give words of affirmation and appreciation, yet we all long for them. This may be a new experience, and some may feel uncomfortable having so many positive things said about them. However, it is one of the treasures and benefits of being in a community of friends in Christ Jesus.

Gift-giving is another way of expressing appreciation. Before the appointed time, talk about this idea with the group so that they have time to make or find appropriate gifts. Another way to do this is to have people write out notes of appreciation for each other and then bring them to the meeting and read them.

When a small group I was in ended, Dixie gave me a rose heart that I had admired in her room. That heart sits on my coffee table and is a visual reminder of God's gift of friendship to me.

Celebration is remembering what God has done in the group and in individuals. Give group members a week's notice so they can reflect on this. Then come together and take time to tell of God's faithfulness and work, even work that is still very much in process.

My favorite celebration comes from Joshua 4, where the Israelites bring stones and build a memorial to God's faithfulness. Give everyone a rock, not a huge one, but big enough to write or draw on. Have each person make a symbol of what God has done for them through the small group. It could be a Bible verse, a picture or a word. At the meeting let each person tell what they have put on their rock and what it means to them, and then have them put it on a growing pile. Conclude with prayers of joy and thanksgiving. Then have people take their rocks home. I still have one from five years ago.

However you decide to remember and celebrate, end with prayers and praise. This is a great way to send each other out in joy, especially if this group will not meet again. You may want to pray Paul's prayers for each other, inserting your own names.

> And this is [our] prayer [for you, Margaret,]: that your love may abound more and more in knowledge and depth of insight, so that you may be able to discern what is best and may be pure and blameless until the day of Christ, filled with righteousness that comes through Jesus Christ. (Philippians 1:9-11)

In this phase the leader returns to taking a lot of initiative, planning evaluation, appreciation and celebration. Don't wait until exam week for this. Most people are too tired and preoccupied. Choose a time the group can leisurely reflect without distractions. As in all phases, the leader takes care to appreciate what people say and affirm people where they are in their journey with the Lord and each other.

When a small group I was in for two years had its final meeting, the leader planned time for us to express appreciation for each other. I was one of the first to receive the appreciation. It felt awkward initially; then I was moved by what my friends noticed and were thankful for about me and God's work in me. Some things I wasn't even aware that God had been doing until that moment.

When my turn was up, I realized that one person had not said anything to me. While my relationship with that person had not been particularly close, there hadn't been any tension that I was aware of either. I was hurt that he couldn't drum up even one thing to say. *Well, I just won't say anything about him either!* I thought.

Then the Holy Spirit got to me, and I found myself asking God to give me one honest thing to appreciate about this guy who had publicly hurt me by his silence. Suddenly, I thought of one thing, then another and another. When it was his turn, I had more words of appreciation for him than anyone else. It was an exciting moment. A holy moment! This was the beginning of a friendship for us as we chatted companionably over dessert after the meeting. It wouldn't have happened if wrap-up had not been planned.

June 30: I miss the group. I was their leader, but I was really just one of them too. They taught me so much. The tough weeks were worth it! There is a big hole in my life without them. Even the folks who bugged me. Hmmmm! I wonder who God will bring next year. I'm praying for them already, even though I don't

The Leader's Needs

Remember that it is God who began a good work in your small group, and it is he who will be faithful to complete it. God knows where each one is in the journey of knowing and following Jesus and in being able to receive his grace and demonstrate his love to others. You live within the tension of trying to help your group move along the journey through phases and the fact that the Holy Spirit is responsible for personal growth and spiritual friendships happening. Don't feel guilty if you didn't get through all the phases. God knows what he wanted to give and accomplish. He knows the barriers and struggles that are deeply hidden. Love and pray for your group's members. Delight in God's love for you and your friends.

Phase	Start-up	Shake-up	Live-it-up	Wrap-up
Member's thoughts	Can I find friends here? What are the purposes of the group? What's expected of me?	Can I be more honest? How can I influence the group? Will this group really work? So-and-so irritates me.	I like and trust this group. I'm committed. These are my friends. Let's go for it and do something.	Was it worth it? How have I grown? What have I learned about God, myself, others?
Member's feelings	Hopeful anticipation. Doubts and fears. Ambivalence.	Anxiety. Impatience. Low enthusiasm. Growing commitment.	Secure in relationships. Freedom and enjoyment. Growing appreciation of diversity.	Joy. Sadness. Reflection.
Member's behavior	Cautious conversation. Safe topics. Giving information.	Decreasing openness and/or increasing openness. Expressions of irritation. Sporadic attendance. Demonstrate commitment.	Express positive feelings. Give honest feedback. Contribute ideas, gifts and leadership. Serve one another.	Laughter. Tears. Delight in friendships.
Leader's attitude and approach	Set tone of openness and acceptance. Create safe atmosphere. Communicate clearly.	Encouragement. Active listening. Hang in there—this is a normal process.	Keep goals clear. Challenge to risk. Encourage group to take initiative.	Reflection. Affirmation. Thankfulness.
Leader's planned activities	Self-descriptive get-acquainted exercises. Set ground rules. Communicate your excitement and hopes.	Trust-building exercises. Manage conflict. Help clarify and redefine commitment.	Develop gifts of others. Delegate. Give feedback.	Activities for evaluating, celebrating, appreciating.
Leader's feelings	Excitement. Anticipation. Energetic.	Enjoying process. Discouraged, frustrated.	Joy and satisfaction. Left out, unappreciated.	Thankfulness. Degree of disappointment.
Leader's needs	Encouragement, prayer, affirmation.	Problem solving with others. Review phases. Prayer support.	Awareness of own feelings as ownership grows. Support of other SGLs.	Evaluating, appreciating and celebrating with other leaders and SGL coordinator.

This chart is adapted from Judy Johnson in *Small Group Leaders' Handbook* (1985), p. 57.

know their names. It will be great to have Carlos as a co-leader and Libby leading worship. Lord, I pray that our friendship as a leadership team will be an example to the people you bring and that they will want to take the journey to becoming a community of friends following Jesus.

Understanding the Chapter

Study

1. Read 1 Peter 5:1-11. What is the leader's main task?
2. List attitudes to develop and ones to avoid.
3. What are leaders responsible for? not responsible for?
4. What hope and encouragement for leaders do you see?
5. What are the rewards of leading a small group?
When do they come?

Reflect

1. Think about your current small group. Describe the relationships and behaviors you observe.
2. Review phases of a small group's life. Which one most closely resembles your group, and why?
3. Which best reflects your group:
    a. we're moving along
    b. help, we're stuck
    c. in a slump
    d. o.k., but . . .
4. Where do you get your support, encouragement, prayer and counsel?
5. Who is praying for you as you lead? If no one is committed to praying for you, decide who to ask.

Apply

1. What would you like to see develop next in your group?
2. What barriers are there to moving through your current phase?
3. Look up the appropriate phase in the community section of *Small Group Idea Book* and select two activities to help your group keep moving on the journey.

8/CULTIVATING GROUP OWNERSHIP
■ Doug Whallon

For the last six weeks, Gino has been faithfully leading his small group. While people have begun to get to know one another, an awkwardness still exists when the group gathers. The studies of Scripture have been reasonably good, but the sharing times and prayer times have been pretty stiff and superficial. So when Gino suggests that the group host a special outreach in the dorm, it is not particularly surprising that the responses of the different persons are mixed, with many being unenthusiastic. Gino can't figure out what's wrong with his group.

By listening closely to the conversation both during the group meetings and around the edges, we can pick up a few clues. As Linda leaves her dorm room to go to the meeting, she tells her roommate, "See you later. I am going to Gino's small group."

While people are still gathering for the meeting, Rob tells another member, "I preferred last year's meeting location to where his [Gino's] meets."

During the discussion of the possible outreach, another member speaks up and says to Gino, "Your group simply isn't ready for this yet."

The problem becomes even more clear when we note what the members of a group which is led by Naomi are saying. As Anne departs her room, she says to her friends, "Gotta go. Our small group meets in ten minutes." Or as the group is still gathering, Phil says to another member, "I liked last year's meeting place better; we should look around for an alternative." As Anne leads the discussion on a possible outreach event, Bert says, "Could we wait till after midterms? We need more time to get ready."

The Difference Is Everything

What is the difference between the two groups? Gino's group still draws its identity from its leader. It is referred to as "Gino's group." In Naomi's case, it is referred to with an entirely different set of words, such as *our* and *we*. Naomi may have launched the group, but a process has occurred within it so that now the group members feel that it is their group.

The subtle shift in word choice reflects a profound difference. A healthy small group develops a common commitment, with each person assuming ownership and responsibility for the group's well-being. Our goal as leaders is to join people together in a significant team experience, not simply to surround star leaders with a collection of individual followers. Each leader should aspire to have a reputation for having a great small group, not for being a great small group leader.

In a group with widespread ownership each person is important. Each is taken seriously. Each has a voice and a perspective, and it matters that everyone is listened to. But within the group, people learn to trust God and one another in order to focus on who they can become together. Over time, shared ownership and group identity develop, especially as the leader learns to cultivate and encourage it. As a result, all the group members have a strong commitment to one another and to the group.

Initial Expectations

Imagine it is September and you are invited to join the newly forming small group in your dorm. You and a half dozen others arrive for the first group meeting. After a brief round of introductions, the person who appears to be taking the lead asks: "What do you want this group to be like? I'll do whatever you want." What do you think will happen? In 99 out of 100 small groups that begin that way, the group will experience polite chaos, followed by a stage in growing frustration, before disbanding in disillusioned confusion.

It is premature to expect the group members to formulate the plans and set the direction at the beginnings of a group. In the initial meetings, the leader needs to help people focus on getting to know one another. There often is value in taking a simple inventory of people's expectations by asking the people about their hopes, but the purpose of such a question in the early going is to better understand where people are coming from, not to have a long discussion that is direction-setting.

For the first few meetings the leader has the responsibility to communicate his or her hopes for the group. For the many participants with

Taken from *Reborn to Be Wild* © 1993 by Doug Hall and used by permission of InterVarsity Press.

"Did Jim *really* leave the group because of a scheduling conflict, or was it because we couldn't accept a non-rodent?"

unclear or undefined expectations, this will set the stage for them. Very likely, many will adopt these as their own expectations. The leader is gently leading by helping the group reach a shared perspective.

Therefore, it is terribly important that leaders take the time to think through their hopes for the small group. Use the four components for a basic framework. Take some time to write them out and then practice saying them aloud so that you can state them clearly. If new members come in later in the group's life, you will want to communicate your hopes to them as well. By stating some initial hopes for the group, the leader is serving the group by:

☐ allowing the group members to focus their energy on building relationships,

☐ protecting the group from conflicting viewpoints,

☐ giving the group an initial direction,

☐ setting the stage for the time when it will be appropriate for the group to determine much more of its own life,

☐ and, since most fellowship groups have expectations for all their small groups, ensuring that those expectations are implanted in the group from the beginning.

Patterns of Small Group Interaction

A sociogram is a fancy name for making a diagram that plots the flow of interaction between people in a group. Try an experiment. During a group meeting, when another member or your co-leader is leading, or shortly after the meeting has concluded, make a diagram of your group. Each circle represents a member. Darken the circle of the one leading. Now draw lines or an arrow from the person talking to the next person who talks. Keep doing this for five to ten minutes. Each line from a circle represents the number of times the person spoke up. Do you observe any patterns?

In a classroom lecture or *monologue* it is usually the professor only who is speaking. The others are either listening, taking notes or sleeping. If you or another in your group is doing all the talking, then your group's sociogram features lines emanating from one source. This can be an effective way to disseminate information, but it is a lousy way to build an involved group and a strong team.

If a teacher engages in a question and answer period, a new pattern of interaction occurs. The question and answer style is a give-and-take or

(continued on next page)

Guidelines for Initial Meetings

The leader will also greatly help the group if some ground rules are provided from the start. These commonsense insights help people to develop good group manners and build healthy relationships. The following ground rules are adapted from *Recovery from Distorted Images of Self* by Dale and Juanita Ryan.

1. Realize that trust grows over time. If opening up in a group setting is risky, realize that you do not have to share more than what feels safe to you. However, taking risks is a necessary part of developing community. So do participate in discussion as much as you are able.

2. Be sensitive to the other members of the group. Listen attentively when they talk. You will learn from their insights. If you can, link what you say to the comments of others so the group stays on the topic. Also, be affirming whenever you can. This will encourage some of the more hesitant members of the group to participate.

3. Be careful not to dominate the discussion. We are sometimes so eager to share what we have learned that we

(continued from last page)
dialogue format where two people at a time are interacting. In your small group, if the majority of the conversation is occurring between only two members, then the sociogram depicts a dialogue. This can be helpful if one of the people is seeking special help or counsel, but again it represents a low level of group participation, and in fact may reflect the rest of the group's disinterest.

In the classroom if more than one student gets involved in the exchanges with the teacher and numerous questions or comments are being fired at the professor, each of which elicits her answer, then what is occurring is a *complex dialogue*. The basic interaction is between two individuals, not the group. It is just that one of the individuals (the student most likely) keeps being replaced by a different student. The professor continues to be the other participant. Such a pattern of interaction often occurs in a small group when the small group leader is either asking all the questions or answering all the questions. The sociogram would depict lines coming from many group members, but every other line would be coming from the leader. While participation has increased, it

(continued on next page)

do not leave opportunity for others to respond. By all means participate! But allow others to do so as well.

4. Expect God to teach you through the passage being discussed and through the other members of the group. Pray that you will have a profitable time together.

5. We recommend that groups follow a few basic guidelines, and that these guidelines be read at the beginning of each discussion session. The guidelines, which you may wish to adapt to your situation, are:

a. Anything said in the group is considered confidential and will not be discussed outside the group unless specific permission is given to do so.

b. We will provide time for each person present to talk if he or she feels comfortable doing so.

c. We will talk about ourselves and our own situations, avoiding conversation about other people.

d. We will listen attentively to each other.

e. We will be very cautious about giving advice.

f. We will pray for each other.

The goal of these ground rules

(continued from last page)
is likely that group ownership is mild.

Discussion takes place when a number of people contribute to the flow of interchange. In smaller settings, such as seminars, discussion becomes an important part of the learning process. The professor will make several opening comments and ask an initial question. Then the students will begin to engage in discussion. In terms of the sociogram, lines are going from one member to another, and many participate in a free-flowing fashion.

Discussion helps a group reach a new level of maturity. For instance, members are better able to counsel and comfort those in pain. During the Bible study, several different members might offer valuable observations about the passage. Then members identify places for application in their own lives. The leader is the catalyst and guides through pivotal moments but is not the epicenter of the group. The group is listening well and avoiding chaos, and overall ownership of the group is extremely high. While discussion may not be the format for wrestling with complex theological questions, this communication style suggests the emergence of a strong community of Christians.

is to create an environment where people are free to be themselves and, in the context of God working among us, to experience a deepening biblically functioning community. These are not arbitrary do's and don'ts, nor are these meant to be simply rules and regulations. Help your group realize the guidelines will help in developing its potential.

If you are going to lead a group whose members have never been a small group before (for instance, for many freshmen, the idea of small groups may be brand new and somewhat threatening), take time to express the importance of being at the first few meetings of the group. Even if they are only "trying out the group," ask potential members to come to the first four meetings before deciding. Without regular attendance relationships cannot bloom. Sporadic attendance virtually assures dissatisfaction. If you are on a campus that has more than one fellowship option, it may be premature in the early fall to push an undecided student toward a multi-week commitment. However, don't hesitate to explain the value of a good start.

Growing Partnership

One of the best examples of a biblical leader who developed group ownership can be found in the apostle Paul. It is tempting to think of him as a high-powered individualist who charged around the Roman world doing great things for God—all by himself. But when we examine what the Scriptures say, we realize that was not so.

Three convictions shaped Paul's whole approach. First, Paul valued all people. Second, he realized that every Christian had something to contribute to the lives of other Christians. Third, Paul saw the potential impact in building Christians together in teams for ministry activity.

For the first part of his life, Paul categorized people as winners or losers, depending on their commitment to living according to Jewish law. After his conversion, his perspective was radically altered by God's perspective. Paul saw God's love for all peoples, Jew and Gentile, rich and poor, male and female. As a result, he dedicated his every action to communicating the life-transforming message of Jesus Christ to everyone he came into contact with. As he wrote to the Corinthians: "For the love of Christ urges us on, because we are convinced that one has died for all" (2 Corinthians 5:14 NRSV). While the campus may write off someone as a loser, a weirdo, a failure or a jerk, God's compassion and love call us to adopt a countercultural perspective and approach.

Paul also prized his relationships with other Christians as gifts from God. Before ever traveling to Rome, he wrote the people in the church: "I long to see you so that I may impart to you some spiritual gift to make you strong—that is, that you and I may be mutually encouraged by each other's faith" (Romans 1:11-12). Even though Paul was the gifted apostle and was equipped for undertaking the most demanding of ministries, he understood the reciprocal nature of relationships—even those with the newest or youngest Christians.

Similarly, everyone in our small groups has something to learn and something to contribute. Paul says in 1 Corinthians 12:7, "To each one the manifestation of the Spirit is given for the common good." We should involve group members in leading according to their interests, gifts and abilities.

Getting Members Involved

There is no doubt that people like to help. Even before you know people enough to discern their primary gifts, invite people to make nonthreatening but useful contributions. Someone might type up the phone list. Another could reserve a meeting room or arrange chairs or bring cookies. You could ask someone to lead in prayer the following week. These seemingly small involvements help people feel appreciated, increasingly at ease and more committed to the group.

Some small groups have "designated roles" which are assigned or chosen early in the group's life, such as host, time keeper, prayer leader or refreshment coordinator. The benefit is that from almost the beginning each person has a function. However, many groups find this awkward. They prefer a more relational approach where involvement grows as gifts are discerned over time.

Ask yourself: What are the gifts and abilities of the different people? Does Mary like to read aloud? Is Bill willing to drive his car to help

Martin, who needs a ride? Does Francis enjoy offering hospitality and putting people at ease? Do Curt and Jack have a good apartment for a group dinner? Is someone good at answering the questions that non-Christians ask? As the leader, ask God to give you insight as to people's natural aptitudes and interests, as well as their resources and their spiritual gifts.

Consider the group needs or ministry opportunities that you can match people with. Does someone need prayer? Would Mario be willing to spend some time talking and praying with that person? Is the group interested in volunteering at the local soup kitchen? Would Jean and Linda be good people to investigate that as a service option on behalf of the group?

Sometimes out of lack of confidence, or simply modesty, people will be hesitant to step forward and participate. As a leader, how can you coax them or what can you do to free them to step forward and serve? Take the time to involve others and then be sure to give affirmation.

Called to Commitment

As Paul was involved in the lives of many Christians, there were some that he sought to call into a deeper level of partnership with him and his mission of declaring the gospel and establishing churches around the Mediterranean basin. Initially, Paul partnered with Barnabas, and they traveled and preached together. In Acts we find Paul inviting others, such as Silas, Luke and Timothy, to join with him. It is fascinating to observe what Luke writes about Paul's traveling companions as the group is expelled from Ephesus after the riot in Acts 19: "He was accompanied by Sopater son of Pyrrhus from Berea, Aristarchus and Secundus from Thessalonica, Gaius from Derbe, Timothy also, and from the province of Asia Tychicus and Trophimus" (Acts 20:4). Clearly, Paul was leading a band of people who were learning to co-labor in the ministry.

One of the best things we can contribute to our small groups is to help them become a ministry team. It a biblical model which multiplies impact. And interestingly, it is often in the context of work done together as a group that relationships deepen.

Over the course of the fall semester, one of the hopes Jay had often voiced in his group was that they would become a team of people that could make a difference in the dorm. One night they determined that they would host a party for their dorm friends as an alternative to the normal Halloween activities. They knew they wanted it to be fun, but also point to the spiritual realities of Christ.

They chose the theme of "masks," asking each of their friends to come wearing a mask of someone or something that they would like to be. Tim designed the invitations. Bill and Ruth arranged for the room and decorations. Soong and Ray bought the refreshments. Ming prepared a five-minute talk about the masks we tend to wear and how Jesus actually frees us to be everything we were meant to be. Together they planned, prayed and prepared.

The party was a wild success. Their friends had a great time. A clear witness of Jesus had been made. To the satisfaction of the small group, the extra work that they had invested resulted in both a valuable outreach and an increased sense of partnership among the members.

Group Agreements

As the group's official leader, I was very pleased with the progress we had made during our first six weeks together. Seven students now seemed firmly committed to the group. They appeared to be enjoying the Bible studies, growing in the depth of vulnerability reflected in their prayers and cautious but open to the idea of attempting an outreach event as a group. The time had come for us to exchange the intentions and hopes that I had laid out in our first few meetings for a set of expectations we determined together.

After an hour's discussion, we reached consensus regarding several group commitments dealing with the four components of our group. We emerged with a strong sense that God had blessed us as a group and was working in our midst in wonderful ways. Even though we still had several difficult times over the next five months together, we had developed a common commitment, something of a common culture and foundation that served us well for the entire year.

Such agreements (or "covenants" in some circles) are important means for developing strong, durable small groups with a high level of group ownership. If you are leading a group for the first time, or if you have never before been part of a group that established a "group agreement," try it. Even in the early going, explain that after a few weeks, it is your hope that the group will draw up some purpose statement.

When a solid level of relational trust has been experienced in your group, suggest that the group devote the next meeting to developing common expectations. Ask people to pray for that process and think about the kind of commitments that they would like to see the group make—and that they would be prepared to commit to—regarding each of the four components. Then, the following week discuss the components and establish what the entire group can commit to. Write down those commitments and have everyone sign them. Celebrate your achievement.

Having a written agreement provides the group with a good tool for accountability. Every few weeks, read aloud the commitments and have a brief discussion as to how the group is doing. Over a stretch of time it is not uncommon for groups to lose their focus or grow sloppy in aspects of their group life. Often, as a result, members will become uneasy with the loss of momentum. These times are critical junctures in the group's life. The group can either continue to deteriorate or can choose to "clean up its act." Your agreement will serve as a backbone for helping your group maintain a high level of satisfaction.

Often it is the leader who recognizes problems or sagging morale. It is much healthier to address it than to pretend that it doesn't exist or hope it'll simply disappear. It takes courage to talk about it with the group, but God will frequently use such frank discussions to trigger a time of spiritual renewal. Go for it; it is worth it!

Understanding the Chapter
Study

1. Read Luke 6:30-46. Even though the initial intent of their withdrawing from the crowd is frustrated, the disciples are given the opportunity to better understand Jesus' mission. In what ways does Jesus help them handle their initial disappointment and build new expectations?

2. How does Jesus use the situation to increase their understanding and participation in the mission?

3. If the disciples had really been perceptive, how could this experience have developed them as a group?

Reflect

1. Think about the most recent small group you were in. To what degree was it group owned?

2. How did you contribute to the life of the group?

3. Whether the group had a formal or informal agreement of purpose, what were the expectations that you and other group members had?

How did those expectations compare with those of the leader?

4. What did your leader do to help the group develop common expectations?

Apply

1. What are your hopes for your group? Consider the four components as you list your hopes. Practice stating your hopes aloud until they become natural sounding. Now you can express them as you invite possible new members or during some of the early group meetings.

2. Make a list of ways that people can help the group even in the first half-dozen meetings. If your group is already meeting, which people will you invite to do what?

3. What team qualities would you like to see develop in the small group?

4. Spend some time in prayer asking God to give you wisdom in cultivating group ownership and commitment in your small group.

9/ENCOURAGING GOOD COMMUNICATION
■ Doug Whallon

Sharon hasn't stopped jabbering since she entered the room, even though no one seems to be particularly interested. Molly and Jean, the most likely targets of her monologue, appear to be exchanging snickers and smirks. Paul, who just deposited himself in the only comfortable chair in the room, seems preoccupied, bragging about his athletic exploits in high school. Bill is politely listening to Paul, but he is clearly uneasy, if not intimidated. Tricia, who has yet to make eye contact with anyone, has found herself a spot on the floor in the room's darkest corner and is silently thumbing through her Bible.

You take a deep breath. As you attempt to invite people to take a seat and begin, the noise and chaos only escalate. Your mind swirls with questions. Will this motley collection of first- and second-year college students ever communicate effectively with one another? Will they ever connect with one another and begin building some kind of community?

Certainly, human nature in its brokenness only guarantees frustration and relational difficulty. But if the Holy Spirit is given room to operate and you understand the principles of good communication, things can begin to happen. The depth of any community is directly related to the quality of communication between members.

Barriers to Communication

Many Christians make the grievous mistake of equating Christian fellowship with standing in small clusters and sipping juice or coffee and munching on cookies while talking about travel, sports and the weather. Our culture has virtually fashioned superficiality into an art form. Perhaps this is an outgrowth of our "doing" orientation, where all that matters is what we have done or achieved in the last two weeks. Or perhaps it is a natural human defense response to protect us from the incessant barrage of media and information that is aimed at our senses.

Madison Avenue, mass media, electronic telecommunications, e-mail, answering machines and faxes—the number of communication forms is multiplying. Information is everywhere, yet there's not a drop to drink to quench our deep-seated relational needs. Increasingly mixed in with noise are voices filled with anger cultivated in troubled families, on overly competitive playgrounds and in front of violent television programs. As a result, more than a few students feel relationally inoculated. Why not turn up the walkman? Why not have the drone of the television supply the backdrop for life? Let the answering machine take your calls. These electronic screens and silencers combine to insulate us from people and allow us to turn off our minds and lower our expectations. Real interaction is too risky and potentially painful. Where is there meaningful communication between people that connects them and spurs their growth?

The Risky Goals of Small Group Life

As small group leaders, we must lead the way to *significant* Christian fellowship, and that is fostered only through meaningful communication between the members. Communication is not simply the flow of information or the exchange of ideas or a set of clever techniques. Rather, it is the kind of careful, caring interaction that provides people with an environment that allows them to admit their failings and needs, to gain courage and support, and to grow and change. "Kingdom communication" enables people to discover that they were indeed created in the image of God, rescued by Jesus from slavery to sin and given the hope and help to change into Christlikeness by the companionship of the Holy Spirit.

Part of the challenge of being a small group leader is discarding the false impression that small group life should be smooth and wrinkle-free. Instead, we are striving to establish patterns of interaction that produce meaningful growth. But for that to occur, negative patterns must be exposed and eliminated.

Where there are sinful problems and relational conflict, we need God to actively redeem the situation and reconcile people. Where there are weak and unhelpful patterns of interaction, we need God to lead us to healthier and health-producing communication. If the communication can become characterized by sincere listening, respecting, caring and helping, then the potential that God can unleash within and through the small group is virtually without limit.

Core Principles of Kingdom Communication

By the time I had reached my sophomore year of college, I had swapped my previous friendly, outgoing manner for a cool sarcasm and a detached cynicism. These were survival mechanisms. As my commitment to and participation in the Christian fellowship grew that year, it became apparent to some Christian friends (more to them than to me) that these "rough edges" were incompatible with God's kingdom. They inhibited my relationships.

Eventually, I changed—or, more accurately, God worked in me. How did this occur? First, several folks became my good friends by spending time with me, listening to me, taking me seriously. Second, their care and friendship became good gifts to me that built me up. Third, within the context of our secure friendship they carefully pointed out how I was "shooting myself in the foot." Fourth, they inspired in me the courage to make some changes that were more consistent with Jesus' design for me. In fact, the care of my friends reflects four biblical principles that we should strive to infuse into the life of our small group.

Listening to others. "You must understand this, my beloved: let everyone be quick to listen, slow to speak" (James 1:19 NRSV). Most of us are the opposite—we are quick to speak and slow to listen. We may listen to teachers, parents, coaches and others in order to gain information and insight. However, we are often slower to listen to our *peers* with the expectation of learning.

Listening is a means of showing interest in and caring for people. While some people may be asking for our counsel, other friends may simply need a listening ear or a shoulder to cry on. We can often give another a wonderful gift of love by patiently listening. For some of us, this requires work to curb our natural tendencies to talk. My wife, Mary, faithfully reminds me on occasions when I am giving advice instead of listening empathetically.

I HEAR THAT ALEXANDRIA HAS A GREAT CHARIOT RACING TEAM THIS YEAR. THEY COULD MAKE IT ALL THE WAY TO THE CIRCUS MAXIMUS. OF COURSE, INJURIES ARE A FACTOR. YOU NEVER KNOW HOW A RACER WILL BE AFFECT WHO THE TAKES...

EVENTUALLY, WOULD-BE DISCIPLE LEONARD CHOSE TO SEEK ANOTHER SMALL GROUP.

Thumbing through the Gospels, you'll often see Jesus asking probing, caring questions. Asking good questions of small group members is one way to develop your listening skill. To get started you might take some time each week to pray about each group member with the intent of discerning the best questions to ask.

Good questions show interest in who a person is: backgrounds, activities, roommates and dreams. Eventually, as friendship builds and the trust level deepens, the person will move from describing the facts of their life to divulging the more central issues, feelings, fears and growth opportunities.

Asking questions is a means of making disciples. Through our questions the person begins to reflect on values, hopes and decisions. Choices to follow Jesus become clearer.

Building others up. A central theme in Paul's letter to the Ephesians is the priority of building up the body of Christ. God has given us the responsibility and privilege of entering into one another's growth process. God wants to see that the gifts he gives are used "to prepare God's people for works of service, so that the body of Christ may be built up until we all reach unity in the faith and in the knowledge of the Son of God and become mature, attaining to the whole measure of the fullness of Christ" (Ephesians 4:12-13). There is nothing small about God's expectations for us.

Yet, in a day and age when there are ample illustrations of the dangers of cults and codependency, we need to be reminded that the Bible calls us to be *responsible to* those around us, while avoiding the

Caring Enough to Ask

Good questions are
☐ simple: Where are you from? What kind of community did you grow up in? How did you decide to come to this college?
☐ open-ended: What was your response to our first small group meeting? How is your rooming situation?
☐ personal: How do you like to spend your free time? What is your spiritual background?
☐ nonthreatening (at least initially): What are you most enjoying about the year? What are you looking forward to this week?
☐ stimulating: In what ways do you think we could strengthen our group? How can I pray for you?

tendency to be *responsible for* all their actions, choices and relationships. As Christian leaders, we are responsible to call our group members to the life values and lifestyle consistent with the kingdom. Yet, what if one gets drunk or another sleeps with his girlfriend or another turns her back on the fellowship? We are not to blame. Each makes his or her own decisions. Our job is to call them to repentance and faith.

Building up people is harder than tearing them down. Encourage patterns of communication in your group that bring personal and spiritual growth. This will occasionally include confrontation, but it will most often involve tons of encouragement. Identify and discourage attitudes and interactions that injure people or inhibit relationships. Watch out for biting humor that cuts down members or causes others to clam up. We are both swimming instructors and lifeguards, teaching our groups to relate effectively with one another at the same time we are staying alert to communication dangers that might cause someone to drown.

Just as an individual possesses a self-image, a small group develops a corporate self-image. The guide for our groups should be "Do not let any unwholesome talk come out of your mouths, but only what is useful for building others up according to their needs, so that it may benefit those who listen" (Ephesians 4:29). As members of the group learn to enter into one another's lives, dig into Scripture, make life-transforming decisions and reach out together, the group's self-image will reflect the reality of God in our midst.

Speaking truth in love. The wisdom of Scripture is wonderfully reflected in another of Paul's instructions to the Ephesians: "Speaking the truth in love, we will in all things grow up into him who is the Head, that is, Christ" (4:15). Paul clearly sets his instruction about communication in the context of the overriding goal, which is the fellowship's growing connection with and resemblance to Christ. Communication between Christians that loses sight of this ambition is wayward.

What does it mean to "speak truth"? In the most narrow contextual sense, this means conveying and teaching the truths of the Scripture. However, because of the clear concern about the ethical quality of our speech that surfaces in Ephesians 4:25-32, we probably have the freedom to interpret the phrase in a broader fashion. In other words, we are to tell the truth to one another about many other matters—ranging from the struggles we are having spiritually to the shortcomings of discipleship that we detect. We speak forthrightly and honestly with one another, *but with one condition:* Before we speak, we make sure that our motive is characterized by a desire for the other person's spiritual well-being. It is the precondition of love that protects the other person from ruthless critique and hurtful evaluation. Love distinguishes confrontation that stimulates change and growth from condemnation that results in hostility and despair.

Particularly in the academic world, people become accustomed to arguing and debating. The verbally gifted can engage in hours of argumentative conversation and leave thinking it was fun. Usually this is a "win-lose" pattern. Someone wins the argument, and someone else loses. Speaking truth in love creates a "win-win" situation, and the kingdom of God advances.

There is no doubt that we want all small groups to reach a level of maturity where people can enter into one another's lives and speak truth lovingly. When this happens, people can repent of sin, overcome shortcomings and grow in spiritual maturity. However, it does take time, trust and the security of a loving environment. Without the love factor, even truth-speakers become noisy gongs and clanging cymbals.

Stirring up love and good works. Any group of Christians who gather together regularly can begin with a burst of action that dissipates over time until there is little that is happening inside or outside of the group. The writer of Hebrews 10:24-25 addresses this undesirable potential: "Let us consider how we may spur one another on toward love and good deeds. Let us not give up meeting together, as some are in the habit of doing, but let us encourage one another—and all the more as you see the Day approaching." The image of a pool of water on a cold day comes to mind. It would quickly freeze if it wasn't for someone regularly taking a stick, stirring it up and maintaining its fluidity.

Good communication in a small group helps prevent the group from getting lazy or complacent. Some groups become so comfortable in their relationships with one another that they lose touch with the outside world and the need people have to know Jesus. We call this becoming ingrown. Our communication with one another should contribute to our common life but should also stimulate us to minister to the people around us. The small group becomes a place of healing for members so that they can be sent back out to serve; a team of people that ministers to one another so that together they can minister to those beyond.

Making a Difference in Your Group's Communication

When the apostle Paul planted new groups of Christians around the Mediterranean Sea, he devoted much time in his letters instructing the new believers in how to communicate with one another. Some of these groups desperately needed his insight and the Lord's help in speaking and listening to one another. No matter how immature or dysfunctional our group's communication, it can change for the better. Not by bringing in professional therapists, but by letting Jesus get into the middle of our group. There are several ways that Jesus can unleash the gospel message through us, thereby enhancing the group's communication and strengthening community.

Accept people where they are (welcome them). When we meet someone new, do we "size them up" quickly? Is it a relatively easy process for us to de-

Learning to Listen

Some people look like they are listening, but they really aren't. Others don't look like they are listening, but they really are. Neither approach is good. When we care for people, we want to learn to listen effectively to them. In this way we get to know them better and let them know that we are interested in their well-being.

Tips for effective listening:

☐ Look people in the eye—but don't stare at them.

☐ Ask occasional questions that show interest and clarify.

☐ Observe the speaker's nonverbal communication. It may be telling you more than her words.

☐ Listen for the feelings behind the words.

☐ Resist distractions. Focus on the speaker's train of thought.

☐ Give feedback. Anything from comments to nods to grunts can assure the talker that you are tracking with him. Smile.

cide whether we like them or not? I tend to be the type of person who quickly forms an impression. The benefit of this style is that when I like someone I am usually able to establish a rapport in a relatively short period of time. However, sometimes I misread a person. Often the other person can sense this and feels uneasy with me. The result is the inability or unwillingness to establish a genuine relationship.

It is our challenge to learn to accept people. We want them to sense our interest, warmth and acceptance. This is not the same thing as approving of them, but we are giving them credit for being human beings. After all, it is God who has created them, and he has deemed to make them in his image. They deserve to be treated with dignity. This is one of the true inalienable rights that we should learn to extend to Christian and non-Christian alike.

No one who joins our group will be perfect—not even remotely so. (If there is someone approaching perfection who joins our group, then we better resign before we contaminate her!) Sin and shortcomings will be dealt with, but for that to productively happen, the students in our group initially need to sense God's (and our) acceptance. "But God demonstrates his own love for us in this: While we were still sinners, Christ died for us" (Romans 5:8). It is the context of hearing and, hopefully, experiencing God's love (perhaps most tangibly through the small group's acceptance and love) that we derive the courage and faith to let God deal with our sin.

Affirm people's unique and good qualities. No matter how much damage sin has done in a person's life, there remains at least traces of the image of God. We will most likely gravitate to some in our groups more easily than others. It's quite easy to affirm and encourage these persons. But what about those we don't as easily relate to, or those we dislike? With these people we will have to work much harder and pray that God will work in us. Yet, we can be assured that if we look, we will discover some quality or ability or dimension that reflects God's goodness. Discovering even one such quality will give us the freedom to genuinely affirm that person.

When the member feels genuinely affirmed (not simply flattered), she will feel appreciated and valued by us. She may also be reminded that she is valued by God. As a result, trust will be increased and our relationship will mature. As Peter wrote: "Now that you have purified your souls by your obedience to the truth so that you have genuine mutual love, love one another deeply from the heart" (1 Peter 1:22 NRSV).

When I was a senior in college, God nudged me to bring together a motley crew of freshman and sophomores who were on the fringes of our fellowship. Phillip, one of the sophomores, frightened me because I was struck by how totally different we were from one another. In fact, it seemed we were polar opposites.

Phillip came from the highly cultured background of an elite prep school. He spoke with the precision and eloquence of a college literature professor. He was a concert-caliber organist. In his teen years he had launched several successful business enterprises. To top it off, when Phillip went to his classes, he wore a white shirt and tie. On the other hand, my background was very plain and middle class. I enjoyed my passion for sports and preferred to blend in with most of my classmates, dressed in jeans and sweatshirts. What did we have in common?

I sought out Phillip so that we could have a few meals together. He talked about his background and several of his struggles. I became very impressed with his commitment to care for people, as he gave generously of both his possessions and his expertise. I found much about Phillip that I liked and could affirm. Over the next months, God built a real friendship between us. To God's glory, that friendship continues some twenty years later.

Actively influence and effect change in people. God's vision for each person in our group is that they become totally transformed, so that they deeply resemble Jesus. That is asking a lot, but the small group context is a wonderful place for God to nurture people in this growth process. As small group leaders, it is our awesome privilege (and sometimes our unnerving responsibility) to be a catalyst stimulating this process. Our vision for the development of our group must not be any less than God's.

The ongoing life of our groups will include a steady diet of the growth nutrients of Bible study, prayer and fellowship. We should also be on the lookout for special opportunities or teachable moments when a member can learn something else about God's character or about being a disciple of Jesus.

Sometimes these teachable moments come after a quiet time of reflection, but more often I find that they come during a time of trouble, discomfort or decision-making. Decisions about how to use summers or what to do with money or how we interact with roommates are excellent windows for seeing operating goals and values. If we can discard the old and adopt the kingdom mindset and patterns, then deep, lasting change will begin to occur. It can be very satisfying to help someone wrestle through an issue, choose a different perspective or decide to act differently.

It is with regret that I remember when one student came to me overwhelmed with his failure in his sexual conduct. I listened to him and proceeded to assure him of God's forgiveness and healing. In my eagerness to offer comfort, I failed him by not spending more time with him to help him sift through his brokenness and clarify his motives. I wonder if a slower, more thorough process might have been more redemptive in demonstrating both the extent of his sinful brokenness and his need for the healing grace of Christ. If we are going to have the fullest effect in encouraging change, we will have to help people deal straightforwardly and honestly with the messy parts of their lives.

We must be willing to express the Scriptural truths and principles of rebuking, correcting and training in righteousness. It is quite possible that in addressing some of the more complex problems in a person's life, we will help them press their discipleship to a new level. At times the door for our influence in their lives will begin with our challenging or even confronting them.

Model honest, vulnerable communication. This can be a challenge for either experienced or inexperienced leaders. It is all too easy to be preoccupied with details ranging from seating arrangements to how to respond to Bill's arrival thirty minutes late. It is sometimes harder to be vulnerable because of role expectations (yours or the group's). Veteran leaders may be inclined to rely on past experience and success and, as a result, not communicate as openly.

If you are feeling nervous about leading a Bible study, however, it is okay to admit it. If you have failed to adequately prepare for the meeting, confess it to the group and ask their forgiveness. If there appears to be a tension growing between several members, your role may be to acknowledge publicly what you have observed in the hope of precipitating resolution. Or perhaps you are experiencing anxiety about schoolwork or are suffering through a conflict with a friend. You don't need to pretend you are perfect or have it all together.

Vulnerable communication requires risk-taking and faith. If we want our groups to be characterized by the kind of communication that leads to good growth and community, then we should be prepared to model it.

Initiate reconciliation. If the group has reached a level of maturity but fallout seems to have arisen between certain people, it may be appropriate to address the issues within the group context. Sometimes, however, we will want to take initiative with people in a more private context to try to understand their feelings and the nature of the problem. In either case, we will probably need to intervene. Our goal is to bring the peace of the gospel to bear—not simply eliminating war, but fostering relational health. God delights in redeeming difficult and broken relationships— which is exactly what the next chapter focuses on.

Understanding the Chapter
Study

1. Read Acts 6:1-7. The early church faced many challenges surrounding its growth and development. When these challenges were handled poorly, they became problems. When they were handled well, the challenges became opportunities for increased ministry. This pivotal passage in Acts shows both kinds of response. What poor communication patterns occurred?

2. What effects on the church might this situation have had if it had continued?

3. How do the Twelve address the problem?

4. What are some of the good communication principles that they model?

Reflect

1. What qualities would you hope would characterize a small group of which you were a part?

2. In your most recent small group, how would you evaluate the quality of communication between the members? What were some of the weaknesses? some of the strengths?

3. How did the leader help or hinder the group communication?

Apply

1. Prepare a few questions that you'd like to ask each of your group members to get to know them better. Show your interest and care for them by asking them the questions.

2. Ask God to help you identify one special quality or gift that each member of your group brings. Thank God for that person and his or her particular strength. Look for a good time to affirm each person either within the group or more privately, depending on which would be most helpful to the person.

10/REDEEMING CONFLICT
■ Doug Whallon

The small group discussion had been spiritually fruitful. As the leader, I was feeling pretty satisfied; to me, the trouble seemed to come out of thin air. One of the group members, Joe, brought the group discussion to a grinding halt—and I was the one in the process of being ground up. The group was in danger of crashing.

I felt threatened as a leader and was deeply disturbed about the setback in our group life. I could have dealt with the "troublemaker" decisively and harshly. That would have made me feel better, while ensuring the demise of the group or at least setting it back even further. Instead, I asked Joe several caring questions. However, his feelings were too raw to get a clear idea of the problem. It would have been ideal to resolve this crisis immediately and in the group context since the explosion had affected us all. But we had to let some time pass.

Within several days, Joe and I were able to discuss the volatile conflict and the ingredients that had triggered it. I took the initiative to express my appreciation for him and told him how important our friendship and partnership were to me. Joe acknowledged that the pressures in his life had made him much touchier than usual. Furthermore, I had been insensitive to his needs. We were able to review this together, confess our particular failings to each other, forgive each other and hug. Just as a broken leg becomes strongest at the place where it has mended, our relationship had become stronger than ever.

But not all was done. Since the group hadn't been present for the reconciliation, we began our next meeting by explaining how God had redeemed the conflict. As a result, our group not only survived the conflict, but became stronger.

Resolution Versus Redemption

Lengthy books and expensive seminars devoted to "conflict management" attempt to teach people to avoid conflict through sensitivity and diplomacy. When conflict occurs, they teach how to extinguish it quickly while exercising damage control. Much of the perspective is drawn from the great cultural ethic of avoiding pain and maximizing gain.

Many people have chosen to adopt low expectations when faced with conflict. They think that they are making peace when they are simply avoiding or ignoring problems. This style condemns relationships to remain superficial.

One of the most painful societal problems our culture confronts is racial tension and misunderstanding. Yet it is often dealt with by offering only Band-Aids for deep wounds. Until the underlying issues of attitude, motivation and control are addressed in the context of daily relationships, there is little prospect for deep healing.

These secular approaches to conflict resolution are impotent impostors for Christ's approach of conflict redemption. What is impossible for people is possible for God, for he specializes in redeeming hopeless situations, defeated people and broken relationships.

The Pain of Conflict

Only a masochist would find pleasure in conflict. Some people do like to debate, and they enter into a kind of verbal sparring with eagerness, failing to realize that it is not a similarly enjoyable experience for the other person. Conflict carries a cost—emotionally, psychologically and relationally. Artificially created conflict rarely seems wise.

The sources of conflict are wide-ranging. Conflict can result from unclear expectations or unintended consequences. For instance, if a member doesn't properly understand the announcement regarding the time for the group's upcoming party, she may feel hurt or left out if she ends up missing it. At the other end of the spectrum of conflict causes is anger or meanness. It is a more blatant manifestation of sin because it intentionally seeks to hurt a person and disrupts a relationship.

Poor communication skills, personal insecurity, troubled family backgrounds and low expectations can all be contributing factors that magnify interpersonal problems. Lots of people have acquired bad habits in conversation such as not listening closely or failing to appreciate the other person's underlying feelings or even just interrupting. Simple things like tiredness or poor health make people more irritable. On the larger scale, it is important to realize that there are different cultural approaches to conflict. For instance, people from Asian cultures are often much less confrontational than those from the more aggressive American culture.

Some people will avoid conflict at all costs. If someone grew up in a family that never argued, then that person might find conflict extremely disorienting or threatening. Or if the person was raised in a family where conflict was constant and never was healthily resolved, that person is likely to have a deep-seated fear of anything that even hints at such a possible problem. They withdraw or accommodate others rather than entering into the zone of discomfort that surrounds disagreement. As a result, they may repress their feelings or submit to the temptation to gossip about the problem or even become emotionally overburdened. Just as being overly combative is unhealthy, so also is the pattern of conflict avoidance.

The Potential Benefits of Conflict

Walter, who was in our college fellowship, seemed to me to be abrasive, obnoxious and arrogant. Since I found myself irritated by his mere presence, I studiously avoided him. You won't be surprised to know that he wasn't that impressed with me, either. I remember feeling quite justified in my assessment of him and must have expressed it to one of the fellowship's leaders.

One Sunday afternoon, two of the leaders came to my dorm room to ask me to serve on next year's leadership team. My stomach dropped when they told me that they were also inviting Walter, and they wanted me to "work on" my relationship with Walter. In fact, they said that they were intervening for his sake, my sake and for the sake of the fellowship.

As a result, Walter and I comitted to having a weekly dinner together just to learn more about one another. I found myself becoming less judgmental of several of his characteristics. Our mutual appreciation began to increase. We became friends and eventually strong partners. The reconciliation that was induced by the intervention of several fellowship leaders became a spiritual gift to me and Walter. Two years later he asked me to be a groomsman in his wedding.

Let's be clear. Unresolved conflicts are liabilities. Few things undermine a group faster than when several members grow frustrated with one another. However, when we allow God to bring peace and health to relationships, there is great gain.

How to Confront

As small group leaders, much of our energy will be invested in encouraging, affirming and building up others. However, on occasion it will be important to confront a member—for his or her sake, as well as for the benefit of the group. This is never fun, but it is necessary. Paul reminds the young leader, Timothy, that Scripture is "useful for teaching, rebuking, correcting and training in righteousness" (2 Timothy 3:16). Furthermore, Paul tells Timothy that the Lord's servant should correct opponents with gentleness (2:25). So, confronting others is a dimension of wise, godly leadership. Here are a few things to keep in mind.

☐ Pray that God will clarify the issues and give you courage, love and insight.

☐ Remember the goal—to help someone grow or change. It is not to unload our frustrations. Double-check your own motives to make sure that it's not because your ego has been hurt.

☐ Go directly and speak personally using language like "I think . . ." or "I feel . . .". In this way you show that it is your message rather than confus-

(continued on next page)

In Walter's and my case, the benefits were threefold. First, we each had a new friend. Second, we learned to become good members of the leadership team. Third, our friendship was an encouragement to other Christians and a witness to a circle of non-Christian friends that we shared. A whole host of relationships grew as a result.

As we handle conflict with others, we also grow individually. We come to more clearly understand what motivates our actions and what values underlie our relationships. This discovery process can be quite humbling, but it can lead us back to greater reliance upon our God. God is in the business of transforming both our relationships and our personal character. He is awfully good at both, if we will let him.

The Process of Handling Conflict

Step 1: Conviction. Before you do anything, you must be convinced of the great value that God places on every person and the quality of their relationships. Paul writes in Ephesians 4:25-27: "So then, putting away falsehood, let all of us speak the truth to our neighbors, for we are members of one another. Be angry but do not sin; do not let the sun go down on your anger, and

(continued from last page)
ing matters by involving others.

☐ Be honest. Don't beat around the bush or be too subtle. Explain in simple terms your concern.

☐ Don't be afraid of feelings and emotions, whether they are positive or negative. Your vulnerability may help the group or person open up. It is okay to say, "I think that you are angry with me. That makes me feel very threatened."

☐ Avoid using questions that imply judgment, such as "Why can't you be on time?" Instead, make statements such as "I get frustrated when you are late."

☐ Keep things in perspective; don't exaggerate. Phrases such as "you always" or "it was the worst" or "you never" are counterproductive.

☐ Ask for feedback: "Is this making sense?"

☐ Describe behavior and don't assume motives. Say, "You often interrupt me," rather than saying, "You won't listen to anyone because you are an insecure egotist."

☐ Help the person make changes. Offer remedial suggestions or creative solutions. Say, "Here is a way you might alter your approach or change your behavior." Pray for the person.

do not make room for the devil" (NRSV). Of course, in my situation with Walter, conviction did not begin with either of us. God gave that insight to several of the group's leaders.

Step 2: Confrontation. This may involve simply acknowledging the existence of the difficulty or the presence of tension. You, as a leader or even as a group participant, may simply say, "I think we are having a problem; let's see how we can resolve it." Or you might say, "We need to take some time to repair our relationships." While another group member might call the group to attend to these matters, often it is the leader who must take the risk of acknowledging the conflict. The best thing that Walter and I had going for us was the wisdom and courage of several very godly leaders.

In the case of problems created by the sinful action or interaction of a group member, the person needs to be confronted so that the sin can be forgiven and overcome. Jesus taught in Matthew 18 how these situations are best addressed. Jesus' approach shows a great regard for human dignity by not unnecessarily shaming a person while simultaneously protecting the

How to Apologize

Leaders often have to apologize more than others. Perhaps it is because leaders are in the middle of the action. There are lots of people with whom to interact and lots of things to do. There are plenty of opportunities for mistakes—the kind that hurt or offend others. Therefore, it is paramount that a leader knows how to receive criticism and, when appropriate, apologize and ask for forgiveness. Here are some things to keep in mind when receiving criticism and apologizing.

☐ Pray for a gentle spirit, a listening heart and an open mind.

☐ Beware of being defensive. Even though it is a natural tendency to want to fight back, dispute or argue, work hard to restrain those inclinations.

☐ Listen. Don't interrupt. In fact, after he or she finishes, ask, "Is there anything else?"

☐ Check what you hear. Put in your own words, without evaluating the content, what you think has been said. If you are unclear, ask questions for clarification. Describe what you perceive the sender is feeling. For instance, you might say, "You are saying that you feel hurt by my actions.

(continued on next page)

people of God and seeking the restoration of the person who has acted sinfully.

Step 3: Clarification. Often it takes a while to figure out what the problem is. This will take some time and discussion and may require postponing the group's usual agenda. Conflict isn't resolved when the issues have been processed if feelings are still injured. You will want to ask how people are feeling at the same time you process the issues together.

As I talked with the fellowship leaders about Walter, they agreed that he had certain shortcomings, but they also spoke up on behalf of his strengths. It helped me that they didn't condemn my perspective, while at the same time their much more positive perspective on Walter helped me to reconsider my opinions. Underneath it all, God was giving both Walter and me a desire to overcome our stubbornness and be at brotherly peace. We started talking during our weekly dinners, and over time suspicion was exchanged for trust.

Step 4: Confession. If people have done things or said things sinfully, then it is critical that they confess their failings to

(continued from last page)
Is that right?"

☐ Determine what the problem or concern is. See if you can get to the point where you agree to the nature of the problem.

☐ Ask yourself what God wants you to learn.

☐ If and when you perceive your failings, demonstrate humility in acknowledging your fault. State your failure or sin and apologize. "I can see now how my insensitivity really hurt you. I am terribly sorry."

☐ Don't just apologize; clearly ask for the other person's forgiveness. If the other person just brushes it off, say it again: "It would mean a lot to me to know that you have forgiven me. Will you forgive me?"

☐ Don't apologize and ask for forgiveness if God hasn't convinced you of wrong attitudes or wrong conduct. This doesn't mean you are not at fault. It may simply mean you need more time to ponder what has been said. You may need to say, "Thank you for raising these issues. I need to think and pray about them. Can I get back to you in several days?"

☐ Thank God for these difficult but helpful opportunities to grow, as well as the chance to improve your relationships with other Christians.

the injured parties and ask for forgiveness. If the injury has taken place within the group context, it is appropriate that the member confess within the group or at least refer to the reconciliation that may have taken place elsewhere. Just as a cut can't heal until it is cleaned, a relationship can't be deeply restored until it is cleansed by the act of confession.

I actually think it was Walter who first asked my forgiveness after we had a half-dozen dinners together and were beginning to enjoy those times. Midway through the meal, Walter leaned across the table and said something like, "I have come to realize that I need to ask your forgiveness for my attitude." He talked; I listened. I knew that there were things that I had to say as well. He listened and graciously forgave me. As the past was dealt with, the potential for the future multiplied.

Step 5: Commitment. When people realize that conflict can be productively handled within a group, their trust in the group grows. It is quite likely that their willingness to identify with the group and invest in its life will increase. It is appropriate for the leader to remind people of how God has guided them through the turmoil and call the people to increased expectation for the ways God will work within the group.

It was clear to the fellowship that God had done a good work in Walter's and my lives. People in the fellowship were encouraged to work on their relationships. Several people outside of the fellowship were also intrigued by the remarkable change and strong relationship that the two of us had.

Conflict and Culture

While Western culture values direct conflict, in many other cultures face-to-face conflict is considered disrespectful. According to Duane Elmer, the author of *Cross-Cultural Conflict,* Asians and Latin Americans may "prefer to approach conflict indirectly." In Spanish "I forgot" ("Se me olvido") "means literally 'It forgot itself to me.' " Elmer continues:

> When I say "I forgot" (active voice), I identify myself as the responsible agent. But that could be embarrassing and cause me to lose face or be shamed. Thus the passive voice is used, suggesting that it happened to me but not implying direct responsibility. And, my face is protected.

When handling conflict in your groups, you will need to consider carefully the different conflict styles that may be represented in the cultural backgrounds of group members. If you are Asian, you may find your indirect method of handling conflict does not get the attention of Anglo group members; they may even think that you are unwilling to deal with the issues. As an African-American leader, you may find that Hispanic group members are hurt and offended when you bring up difficult issues of group life.

Understanding how conflict and culture relate could be a lifetime task, so don't allow yourself to be overwhelmed by it. Neither does this mean that you should gloss over conflict. Just take the time to understand the conflict styles of your group members and be sensitive to them. If you want to know more, you'll find *Cross-Cultural Conflict* (IVP) a big help.

God's Resources for Handling Conflict

In the academic world, we are taught to think critically about ideas. Unfortunately, we carry over that mode of thinking and talking to our approach to people as well. Sometimes we employ our critical abilities to analyze others' weaknesses; other times we engage in tearing others down so as to build ourselves up. Campus fellowships need to be thoughtful about which style of talk they adopt. Is it the language of the culture or the language of the kingdom? Our words should give grace, meaning they point people toward God and his resources, rather than turning them off to him.

Scripture is also filled with models for us to imitate. In Ephesians 4:32—5:2 Paul writes:

Be kind and compassionate to one another, forgiving each other, just as in Christ God forgave you. Be imitators of God, therefore, as dearly loved children and live a life of love, just as Christ loved us and gave himself up for us as a fragrant offering and sacrifice to God.

When we have squabbles in our family, this is the passage we often turn to. From the very core of the gospel, the life and death of Jesus Christ, several pivotal implications for our relationships are highlighted. Just as Jesus loved us and gave himself sacrificially for us, so too are we to lovingly care for one another. Just as God in Christ has forgiven us, we are to forgive one another.

Forgiveness is one of the distinctives of Christianity. It is focused not on what we humans do, but on what God does. God no longer holds our sin against us. He has intervened unilaterally and acted on our behalf. We no longer have to live under a guilt trip. And by the same power of the Holy Spirit that raised Jesus from the dead, we have the God-given power to love and forgive the people around us.

These concepts are clearly taught in Scripture. The power to enact them comes through faith and prayer. The courage to confess sins and ask forgiveness of others, and the power to love and forgive others are to be dynamics of Christian living activated by the Holy Spirit. As a small group leader, whether you are trying to resolve conflict between some of your group members or you are directly involved in the fray, it is essential that you go to God, asking him to work in and through you to redeem conflict.

Troubleshooting with Troublemakers (Without Killing Them or the Group!)

Meet some of my best friends. While they don't try to cause problems intentionally (at least most of the time), they can cause headaches for any small group leader. Here are some ideas for coping.

Michael Motormouth: He talks too much. Sometimes he makes sense, but often what he says is only marginally insightful. When he is excited, he dominates the group and in the process the others become quiet or withdraw.

As the leader, try to sit next to Michael to regulate his participation more easily through eye contact and nonverbal interaction. After Michael speaks, ask the group, "What do others of you think?" If Michael still speaks so much that it is hurting the group, talk privately with him. Affirm his eagerness and enthusiasm. Explain the goal is whole group involvement. Ask him to help by making sure others are involved. If he is the type that always jumps in when there is a second of silence, tell him that silence is okay, and that it is often the doorway leading toward

participation for quieter people.

Wilma Off the Wall: Unfortunately, Wilma's comments often seem unrelated to the topic of discussion. They are disruptive and lead to frustrating tangents. When the group is studying the Beatitudes, Wilma asks about predestination. When the topic is self-image, Wilma focuses on baptism.

As the leader, take a moment to try to discern a possible connection. There may be one in Wilma's mind. If you don't perceive one, don't simply dismiss Wilma's concern. But do find a quick way to get the discussion back on track. Say to Wilma something like this: "Wilma, that is an interesting idea. Since it isn't the focus of today's study, could we explore it later or after the meeting?" You need to be willing and able to intervene in unproductive discussion, otherwise the group's frustration will grow.

Johnny Come Lately: Why does he always show up ten or fifteen minutes late? He is often apologetic, offering every excuse imaginable. He even promises that it will never happen again. But it does. His tardiness is hurting the group's sense of togetherness and morale. The group is almost forced to start again when he finally arrives or to start late—but that makes it hard to do everything the group is committed to.

There is always value in reminding members of expectations for group life. One of those will be to start on time. Unless it is just a question of several minutes, you will be wise to keep starting on time and increasing Johnny's incentive to be there promptly. You may need to address him directly outside of the group or even within the group. If all else fails, then have someone in the small group arrange to meet him and actually accompany (bring) him.

Wanda Wallflower: Sometimes she is so quiet for so long that you even wonder if she is dead. Her silence mystifies many in the group who don't know whether she is disinterested in the discussion or in them or what. The ability of the group to come together is limited by her lack of involvement.

It is possible that Wanda is feeling deeply alienated from the group and therefore has withdrawn. Alternatively, she may simply be a very quiet person or fairly nonverbal. Keep striving to establish an environment that encourages widespread participation. Be quick, but not phony, in affirming contributions. Sit across from Wanda so you can make eye contact and look for nonverbal hints that she has a comment to offer. Only ask direct questions as a last resort.

Dogmatic Dante: He is confident that he has all the theologically correct answers. He holds a hard-line on some rather controversial, debatable issues. Open-ended questions, meant to bring broad participation and thoughtful discussion, are often met by clear, but abrupt, short answers. These answers tend to end the discussion because everyone else is intimidated or afraid of sounding wishy-washy.

Ultimately, Dante needs God to help him develop a new level of humility. You don't want to remove Dante's confidence in Scripture or in the fact that God does have answers for questions, but he needs help in appreciating the complexity that surrounds many questions and many answers. He also needs to grow in valuing the learning process for both others and himself. Point out to him how the group will benefit from taking more time to reach conclusions.

Small Group Life Reconsidered

How shall we think of the ideal small group? Will it be nice and neat like a well-maintained garden? It is a tempting image, especially since it can be so fruitful. But I suspect you already know that the life of a small group can be quite messy. In all truth, even the best of small groups is more like a compost pile.

A compost pile is a small fenced-off area that gardeners set aside for tossing all their organic garbage. Into it they put their grass cuttings, spoiled vegetables, rotten fruit and even egg shells. It is a mix of pretty unappetizing ingredients. It is ugly, and it is smelly. Yet over time, the natural processes of decay and decomposition convert the thrown-away garbage into very rich nutrients. Ironically, it's the nutrients of the compost pile, when added to the garden, that make it fertile and spur on productive growth.

A similar process occurs in a small group. There is a mix of people. They are not all the most attractive people from the campus. Some come with the baggage of broken family backgrounds. Others come with poor self-images or little personal confidence. Some may be laboring under a load of guilt from feelings of inadequacy or moral failure. A few might even have the mistaken impression that they are God's gift to the Christian fellowship. You, as the leader, may feel overwhelmed and underequipped. Yet, over a period of time, as God guides the interaction between the people, good things begin to happen. The group becomes an environment for change and growth. People are transformed and together the group begins to make a difference in their part of the world. Thank God for small group compost piles!

Understanding the Chapter
Study

1. Read Philippians 4:2-3. As wonderful as the church at Philippi was,

it wasn't immune to relational conflict. Paul does not hesitate to deal with the strife between two leaders. In fact, he asks the other leaders to work hard to redeem the conflict. What are Paul's hopes for Euodia and Syntyche?

2. What do you think Paul wants the other leaders to do? Why?

Reflect

1. Recall a relationship that was severely strained but eventually renewed. What changes in attitudes and actions were made?

Which of the five steps discussed in the chapter can you discern having occurred?

2. Are there any relationships within your small group or fellowship that seem to need some divine attention? Pray for those people. Ask God to heal their relationships.

Apply

1. Of the strained relationships in your group are there any in which you think God might want you to be a peacemaking agent? Pray for leading and conviction. How should you proceed?

2. Now for the tough questions. Are you the source of pain or tension in someone else's life? Are you holding a grudge against someone or feeling distant and cold toward someone? Ask God to show you your sin—of attitude and action.

Will you confess to the person and ask for his or her forgiveness? The momentary embarrassment will be well worth the redemptive joy. Take the first step.

PART 4
SERVING AT THE HELM

11/The Growing Leader

12/The Influencing Leader

13/The Organizing Leader

The happy union of technology and accountability.

11/THE GrOWiNG LEaDER
■ Patty Pell

Mike was a dynamic student. From the very first moment of his freshman year he wanted to be involved. He volunteered for committees and showed up at every event. By his sophomore year Mike was a small group leader. But during that year things began to change. He made unwise choices and kept them secret. He became consumed by schoolwork and a relationship with Debbie. He showed up at chapter events less and less. He lost interest in his small group and in what God was doing. Pretty soon his small group disbanded and Mike drifted away from fellowship.

Danya entered the chapter as a freshman with excitement and vision. She got involved quickly and got to know some other women right away. She shared struggles and joys with them throughout the year. As a sophomore, Danya also led a small group. She planned her time during the week, balancing her relationship with God, small group, academics, John and friendships. She loved her small group and saw God do tremendous things throughout the year. The next year she volunteered for leadership again.

The same two paths that Mike and Danya faced are spread out before you. As small group leaders and spiritual leaders in your fellowship, you face the road that can deplete your energy and your vision, leading away from growth and from God. You also face a road that winds toward maturity. This road keeps vision alive and keeps passion from dying. If you know what the road toward maturity looks like, you can recognize it and follow it.

Character Qualities of a Maturing Leader

A leader may have charisma and talent, but if that leader's character is not trustworthy, full of integrity and strong, his or her influence is limited. In the presidential election of 1992 character became a prominent issue of the campaign. "Is character important?" was the question voters dealt with. If we look even briefly at Scripture, we know that the answer to that question is a firm "Yes!" God is interested in who we are as people, not just as leaders.

Identity in Christ. Leading the small group meetings was a thrill and a joy for Jason. He was good at his job, and people told him that all the time. He began to find more and more of his worth in how each week's meeting went and how many students attended. While the small group was doing well, so was Jason. But when the group began to have problems, Jason began to struggle as well.

This is not an uncommon experience for small group leaders. It is far too easy to compare your group to someone else's, to rely on numbers to tell you how you are doing as a leader or find your happiness and self-worth in your position as a leader, rather than in Christ.

I spent one summer teaching an adult Sunday-school class in the book of Esther. I have always loved the book; yet the more we studied it, the more amazed I became at the character of Esther herself. She exhibits so many leadership qualities, only one of which is her solid identity in God. Esther remained loyal to her God and her people even as a queen.

In the same way we will be able to do all that God asks us to only if our self-worth comes from being a child of God. When we falter and allow ourselves to find our worth in the group or in our ability to lead, we will be disappointed and bound to pleasing others rather than God. Be faithful to what God calls you to and let God determine the results of your work.

Integrity no matter what. Esther was faced with some very difficult choices as queen. She was Jewish, and the Jews faced a threat that could have wiped them out. Esther was given the responsibility of approaching the king to ask for his help—risking death. She could have given in to her fear and refused to help. But instead Esther chose what was right. Her beliefs and standards never wavered no matter what the circumstances.

Today we are surrounded by leaders who are the opposite of Esther—constantly wavering and changing allegiances. Yet our private lives and public lives must be consistent. God expects us to live what we teach. If we are to be mature people and leaders, then we must not cheat on homework or tests, lie to a professor, or find a way around the rules of the university. Our honesty must come out when we apply for jobs, meet with other students and answer questions in Bible study. Our integrity must be apparent in our relationships, our attitudes and the way we demonstrate love.

Dietrich Bonhoeffer, a pastor in Germany during World War II, chose what was right. When he left Germany right before the start of the war, he left behind the young Christian people he was discipling and leading. He was in the United States for only a month before he returned to Germany convinced it was not right for him to be anywhere but with those he was discipling and teaching, in spite of the war that was going on. He lived a life of integrity. The things you may face might not be similar to those of Bonhoffer, but there will be plenty of times when choosing right will not be an easy road.

Our character has a tremendous influence on our small groups. If we are inconsistent and dishonest, our groups will feel the impact. Our character is more important to our groups than our techniques and leadership skills.

Your campus will take notice if Christians begin to boldly do what is right without compromise. Students will be drawn to Christ because of the sincerity of the lives they see. And you will grow into maturity as a leader in the work of the Lord.

Living as sheep and shepherd. God has placed us as shepherds over our small groups. Our role is to care, nurture and pray for the sheep in our groups. However, we are sheep too. If we forget this, we are likely to forget that we must allow Jesus to shepherd us. As leaders, we need direction; we need Jesus to give us insight into our group and wisdom in helping others. As leaders, we need to be fed from the wellspring of life so we can give to those in our groups. We do that by being the sheep in God's pasture.

God calls us to follow him. No matter what we happen to be doing in the work of the Lord, this never changes. Following means being open to the counsel of others. God will use small group coordinators, staff-workers, roommates, parents, friends, group members and pastors to teach us. Yes, you are a leader. You will be asked to show the way. But you are also a sheep who follows. Let the Good Shepherd lead you beside quiet waters and down paths of righteousness.

Remember Mike and Danya? Both had leadership skills, but what made the difference in their lives was the depth of their character. Choosing the road of integrity means continually growing in character with your identity firmly grounded in Christ as shepherd and Lord.

Growing Spiritually

Your spiritual life is foundational to your life as a leader. Too many times leaders attempt to carry out their responsibilities without the empowering times of fellowship with God. Small group leaders teach, disciple and lead out of their own knowledge and experiences. When a leader is growing spiritually, there will be overflowing resources from which to draw. However, if a leader becomes stagnant, the reservoir of energy and insight quickly dries up, and the job of leading becomes increasingly more difficult and less fruitful.

The lives of godly leaders in Scripture highlight some of the areas of spiritual life that we must protect and nurture: "My soul finds rest in God alone; my salvation comes from him. He alone is my rock and my salvation; he is my fortress, I will never be shaken" (Psalm 62:1-2). These words come from the heart of King David, and they give us a glimpse of his relationship with God. In the psalms we see David going to God in all circumstances whether he was angry, downcast, overwhelmed, joyous or at peace. David was very intimate with God, and he knew that no matter what happened in life, he could always turn to the Lord.

We cannot teach ourselves truths or comfort ourselves or transform our own lives. All that is the work of God. As leaders, we will fail miserably if we do not recognize the need to go to God at all times. It is crucial for us to set aside regular times to spend alone with the Lord, to sit at his feet like Mary and learn from him, to rest in his presence and be renewed, to listen to his truth and gain correct perspective, and to revel in his power and be strengthened.

A wonderful picture of what it means to meet with the Lord and grow in a relationship with him is recorded in Exodus 33:7-23. Regularly, Moses went to the tent of meeting to be with God. He went alone, and as he entered the tent, the presence of the Lord in the form of a pillar of cloud would settle on the tent. "The LORD would speak to Moses face to face, as a man speaks with his friend" (v. 11). What a glorious scene of God and a man communing together! We have the same opportunity to meet with the Lord and speak with him as a person speaks with a friend. Jesus has made it possible.

The effects of regularly spending time with God are innumerable. For Moses those times renewed his strength, gave him vision and wisdom about what God was asking him to do, and gave him the ability to lead. We all need these things in our lives, especially as leaders. So guard those times of quiet with God selfishly, letting nothing take precedence.

Over the years I have had devotional times that have been spectacular and times that were dry. But I realize that my spiritual growth depends on the quiet moments of prayer, contemplation and Bible study. It is in these times I hear God and my heart is open for change. It is through the times of Bible study that I grow as a disciple of Christ and deepen my understanding of the life of faith. We cannot go without meeting with our Lord and Savior if we want to continue growing spiritually and as leaders.

Watching for God

I had my life all planned out from high school through my junior year in college. Then, at the beginning of my senior year in college someone asked me a very serious question about my career path, and for several months I was in turmoil. Before that moment my plans had been off-limits to God. He could give me some insight, comfort me when I needed it and bail me out of situations, but for him to venture too near my life-decisions was unacceptable. I had not been paying much attention to how God was laying the groundwork for some major changes. My eyes were not on him but on me, and my heart was not waiting with expectation for God to lead. My spiritual growth was tremendously hampered until I opened that tiny hole in my heart to God. That day when my InterVarsity regional director questioned my choices, I entered into a time of spiritual growth that was explosive.

Part of growing spiritually is recognizing that God is constantly speaking to us. He desires to teach us and guide us, and it is when we allow him to do that that we grow in ways we never imagined. Scripture is full of accounts of people who were open to what God was doing. Before Esther took the risk of going to King Xerxes without being summoned, she fasted and prayed. She listened for the Lord's direction.

Another such example is the story of Philip and the Ethiopian eunuch in Acts 8:26-40. Philip had been involved in a successful ministry in Samaria. People were being healed, demons cast out and many were coming to the Lord. But suddenly the Spirit of God sent Philip to a deserted road without instructions. The Spirit then directed him to a chariot that was carrying the Ethiopian eunuch. Philip began a conversation which led to the eunuch's conversion and baptism into the Christian faith. Philip was watching for what God was doing around him and in him. He listened to the Spirit and obeyed when God spoke. Philip grew in his faith and continued to preach the gospel and follow the Lord.

As leaders, we must constantly be in tune to the Lord. As we enter into leading a small group of people that God has brought together, we need to be closely connected to God to hear his direction and follow his lead. When we are watching God, we maintain our vision and our passion, we are strengthened and empowered, and we are used by the Almighty God in his work.

Honesty with God

Ask a few of your neighbors or coworkers about Christian leaders, and many of the responses will reflect the moral failure of prominent leaders in ministry. It is not surprising that the world remembers these fallen leaders. Christians profess moral strength and transformed lives, and yet again and again the world sees the opposite occurring. What makes it so difficult sometimes for Christian leaders to make wise and godly choices? The answers to these questions are not easy, and there are many factors that work together, but one of the common problems is lack of honesty with God.

If we were to list the most horrible sins, murder and adultery would probably top our lists. And King David committed them both. He not only made a terribly foolish choice by committing adultery with Bathsheba, but tried to cover up his sin by committing murder on top of it. He was in the highest leadership position among God's people, and his life was tainted by sin and very serious consequences.

The road through confession and repentance was not an easy one for David. But God offered help by sending Nathan, the prophet, to point out the sin David was hiding from. Being in a leadership role does not exclude us from needing the accountability of our brothers and sisters in Christ. No matter what position we hold or how well our small groups are going, sin will seep in. And when it does, we have two choices. One response is to hide it or ignore it and go on leading. The other response is confession and repentance.

When we choose to hide our sin, we begin to draw away from God. It becomes difficult to spend time with him and difficult to pray. We are plagued by guilt and doubt. Soon our spiritual growth is severely damaged.

Repentance leads to forgiveness, cleansing and relationship. When we confess our sin to the Lord, we experience his grace and renewal. We keep climbing on our journey with God with new understanding and strength-

Accountability 101

1. Ask someone who you respect and trust to be your accountability partner.
2. Ask pointed questions of your friend and be open to receiving them.
3. Be honest with each other.
4. Pray for one another very specifically.
5. Maintain confidentiality!

ened faith. To get back on the path—and stay on it—we get into relationships of accountability to help us resist the temptations that entice leaders.

Jamie couldn't seem to help herself when it came to her roommate's money. It started with taking some change from her desk and turned into frequently taking money from her purse. She was filled with guilt, but was trapped in the cycle. Her times with the Lord became increasingly difficult until she could hardly bring herself into his presence to pray. Yet, to her small group Jamie seemed to have everything together. Finally, the problem became unbearable, and Jamie confessed her behavior to a close friend in the chapter who she trusted and listened to. Jamie's friend responded with grace and encouraged her to confess to her roommate and small group, asking for their forgiveness and help.

We need to surround ourselves with people who we respect and will listen to. We must give them the freedom to ask us about our areas of weakness and struggle. Their role is crucial if we are to mature as leaders.

Even Esther had someone who kept her on the right path and who wasn't afraid of confronting her. Mordecai asked her hard questions and exhorted her when at first she refused to enter the king's presence. Because Esther respected Mordecai, she listened to his wise counsel.

From David we also learn what confession and repentance look like. In 2 Samuel 12:13 David takes the first step by acknowledging his wrongdoing: "Then David said to Nathan, 'I have sinned against the LORD.' " We see his confession in the words of Psalm 51. He lays his sin before the Lord and asks for forgiveness. The psalm is a wonderful picture of confession and the renewal that comes from it. When we sin, our first step is to go to the Lord in humility and confess our wrong.

The road does not end with merely acknowledging our sin. It leads on to repentance. A. W. Tozer describes repentance like this: "To move across from one sort of person to another is the essence of repentance: the liar becomes truthful, the thief honest, the lewd pure, the proud humble. The whole moral texture of the life is altered." For all Christians this is what God desires—a changed life.

Growing Emotionally

Walking through the lobby of my dorm on my way to class, out of habit I checked the mailbox to see, if by any chance, there was something there. Through the tiny door of my box, I saw green engineering paper and smiled because I knew it was a note from a friend in another dorm. He always left me encouraging notes when I was having a rough time.

Maturing emotionally requires times of stretching and struggle when we question who we are and why we're here. However, God has given us his family to support us. A leader needs to have close friends who will encourage, motivate, exhort and listen. One of the most satisfying experiences is spending time with someone who does these things in your life.

As small group leaders, at times we will be discouraged and frustrated. It is in these times that we desperately need a deep relationship. Through friendships, we will be challenged to continue growing in our ability to

SPIRITUAL PICK-UP LINES

respond to our feelings and other people's feelings in godly ways.

A relationship of this kind takes openness and commitment. You will not develop intimacy with a person if you never discuss the real joys and sorrows of life. It may be frightening sometimes. However, taking a few steps in building a relationship like this will show you the tremendous rewards you can receive. God will work through this person to show you his grace, faithfulness, comfort and encouragement. We cannot lead or grow if we attempt to do it alone.

Growing Relationally

One of the hottest workshop topics at our fall conference has always been relationships. Whether we are discussing dating relationships, relationships with friends and roommates, or family dynamics, everyone wants to be in that workshop. I think it is because we all realize that having healthy relationships is difficult. We crave more insight about what a healthy relationship looks like and what to do about an unhealthy one. Leaders must work hard at developing and nurturing the relationships they have so that they reflect holiness. Maturing as leaders requires us to mature in our perspective of relationships and in our behaviors.

Kevin and Tom were both chapter leaders who had girlfriends. Kevin adored Lisa, and they spent hours together. They didn't talk much about their relationship, preferring to "go with the flow" instead. Kevin and Lisa made many unwise decisions, such as staying overnight in each other's rooms, only planning dates where they would be alone and putting themselves in very tempting situations. They were a poor example of a godly relationship. Chapter members began to question their behavior and what was acceptable in a dating relationship.

Tom, likewise, was crazy about Suzanne. But Tom and Suzanne were careful about the physical limits they set. The dates that they planned were not always exclusive, and they left time for other relationships. Many chapter members learned about healthy dating patterns by watching and listening to Tom and Suzanne.

Dating can be a complicated adventure. Society sets up many expectations, and we have few models of truly healthy dating couples. However,

God is concerned about the state of these relationships in our lives. We must pursue holiness.

Beyond dating there are many other temptations that threaten to exert unhealthy and ungodly influences on our relationships. Pornography and other sexually explicit material can wreak havoc on relationships and cheapen interaction between males and females. We need to be very aware of all that we read and watch. Are the movies we watch uplifting and helpful, or do they promote damaging messages about men or women? Will those around us notice that we stand for what is moral and good by the shows we faithfully watch or the books we read? All of these things enter in to what it means to be a Christian leader.

There are many other important relationships in which God wants us to exhibit godliness and healthy patterns. The way we relate to our families is vital. Dysfunctionality in many homes causes us to relate to our parents or siblings in unhealthy ways. God's desire is to work on those areas and restore wholeness. As we allow God to open up more and more areas of our lives and redeem them, we will become stronger spiritual leaders and role models. A speaker once said that the state of our relationships says a lot about the condition of our spiritual lives. I certainly agree! Relating to people in a healthy, nurturing, godly way is challenging. It is

Top Ten Rationalizations Christians Give for Sitting Through an R-rated Movie

10 It's art.

9 I have to learn how unbelievers live.

8 It's okay. One of the characters is a priest.

7 No, really, it *is* art.

6 It doesn't affect me as long as I cross my arms and look displeased.

5 I'm just trying to figure out what they're doing.

4 This might be important to the plot later.

3 My *goodness,* is this artistic . . .

2 I have to count the sex scenes if I'm going to report it to the morality police.

1 It's either sit through this or rent *Chariots of Fire* again.

Taken from *Potluck Hall of Fame* © 1992 by David Dickerson and used by permission of InterVarsity Press.

a lifelong task to identify all the sin in our relationships, but allowing God to show us what he is working on and responding to him is key to our growth. We must make sure as leaders this area of our lives gets significant attention—wise counsel from others, good reading material and guidance from the Lord.

Healthy Living

After Jesus experienced a very tiring day of healing and casting out demons, he rose early the next morning to retreat by himself and pray. On another occasion, when the disciples returned from preaching the kingdom and healing the sick, Jesus took them away to rest. Nehemiah divided the task of building the walls of Jerusalem into small groups. When Moses became exhausted by his heavy caseload, he took Jethro's advice and appointed others to be his officials and serve as judges.

Jesus, Nehemiah and Moses all recognized one of the basics of human life: we have physical limits. Although we know that this is true, we still try to disprove it again and again. At some point, then, the truth begins to take over, and we collapse in exhaustion, sickness, depression or anger. When we do not take care of our bodies by living within our limits, we hinder God's work in the long run because we must quit the race early.

My supervisor reminds me frequently that we are in a marathon and not a sprint, so we must live accordingly. Maturing as a person and a leader involves discovering what your limits are and then working within those boundaries.

Like Moses, we need to listen to the helpful advice we are given. Delegation and surrounding yourself with people who can help you with your tasks is key to effective leadership and crucial to maturity. It allows us to accomplish what we are asked to do and empower others in ministry at the same time.

We need to be constantly seeking the Lord about the vision he has set before us, so that we have the freedom to say no to some things that come into our lives. Very conscientious leaders are frequently plagued with the inability to say no. Instead they fill their schedules to the breaking point with many things that may not be a part of what God's vision is for them.

It is important to know your vision and goals and then stand behind them by refusing to do things beyond your physical capabilities. This will keep you from burning out and will help your spiritual and emotional life remain healthy.

Jesus was keenly aware of taking care of the physical body. He rested when it was needed, and he encouraged others to do the same. If we are to have the energy to be leaders and follow God each day, then we need to start making good choices about our health. If I choose to eat unhealthy food, get little rest at night, neglect exercise and never take time out to play, soon I will be unable to fulfill my responsibilities because of illness, exhaustion or depression.

Too many times we choose to do unhealthy things without thinking of the consequences. Mature leaders make wise decisions. This might mean that you need to rethink how late you stay up talking at night because it will affect the next day and your health. You may need to evaluate your eating habits and whether or not you walk to class to get some exercise or drive. Leadership involves every aspect of life, including the condition of your physical body.

Managing Time

As you think about all the things this book says about leading a small group, chances are that you may be feeling overwhelmed at times. Even thinking about making time to exercise and relax, sleep enough, and eat right may weigh heavily on your mind. Growing as a leader means developing skills in time management and exercising self-control. Having skills in setting up a schedule, organizing your tasks, studying efficiently, planning each week and day, and remembering what is to be done will help you tremendously.

My husband's organizational system involved writing notes down on a scrap of paper and stuffing it into a pocket somewhere. At the end of the day he might remember to clean out his pockets, or he might forget and the notes were sent through the washer. As you can imagine, many dates and meetings slipped from his mind. Recently, he has developed a system to help him organize his life which suits his personality and his needs. An electronic organizer, which beeps to remind him of a variety of things, has made an incredible difference for him.

It may be that all you need to do is think through some of these things and set up a plan. It might be that you have no experience in good time management, and you need a good book, like Gordon MacDonald's *Organizing Your Private World,* or organizer system, like DayTimer, to help. Whatever the first step is for you, I suggest you acquire some skills before you jump into the year with your small group.

God brought you to your school as a student and as his servant. Fulfilling this call requires juggling ministry and school. Most of us waver on the edges of the spectrum, either consumed by school and that 4.0 GPA or taking our academic responsibilities too lightly. Being consumed by academics can lead to missing opportunities to further the kingdom. Neglecting academics is poor stewardship of our opportunity to learn. Managing time between these areas means we must keep our identity straight. Our identity and self-worth comes from being children of God, not our final GPA or the size of our small group.

Kim was not the same person I had met four years before. She slipped into a small group meeting as a freshman, unsure and questioning. Her life was disjointed and her relationship with God just barely beginning. Over the four years she spent in our chapter leading small groups she matured

Tips for Time Management

1. Identify one or two primary goals for the semester (consider spiritual goals, academic goals and so on).
2. Find a useful planning device that works for you, like a calendar or daily organizer.
3. On your calendar put in the non-negotiable items in your schedule that correspond to the goals you made (tutoring sessions, small group meetings).
4. Make lists of things to be done, such as calls, homework assignments, errands and so on.
5. Prioritize the items on your lists according to your goals.
6. Use your unscheduled time wisely. Run a few errands on the way to class, study during that hour between classes and write lists while waiting in line.
7. Stay ahead in your classes—read ahead, finish projects early, start research as soon as possible.

into a quality leader. Her life was a testimony of integrity, honesty and holiness. She was humble and anxious to learn. She was secure in who she was in Christ and was balanced in her time management. Everyone she came in contact with through her small groups was changed because of who she was and her leadership. Likewise, may each of us mature as people and leaders in God's kingdom.

Understanding the Chapter
Study

1. Read Genesis 39. What are all the temptations, pressures and consequences that Joseph faced in this chapter?

2. In what ways does Joseph exhibit some of the character qualities that have been discussed in this chapter?

Reflect

1. Evaluate what God has been doing in your character recently. What areas has he been working on?

What steps might you need to take to grow in these areas?

2. What role do confession and repentance play in our spiritual growth? Spend some time praying and ask God to reveal any areas of your life in which repentance and confession are needed.

3. What is an accountability relationship?

How is it crucial to maturity?

Apply

1. Review the sections on growing emotionally, physically and relationally. Which of these areas in your own life needs some attention right now?

2. What are specific things you can do to address this area?

12/THE INFLUENCING LEADER
■ Nina Thiel

Carolyn was a junior at UCLA. She and others from her Inter-Varsity fellowship moved into the residence halls in order to live out the gospel among fellow students, loving them as Jesus would.

Carolyn began a Bible study in her hall and met a new student named Jenny. Jenny didn't know Jesus and only came sporadically to the Bible study, but Carolyn was impressed by her good questions about Christianity and her eagerness to get answers. Carolyn also found that she really enjoyed Jenny's personality, and she began to hang out with Jenny.

When Jenny wanted to sing and dance down the hallway on the way to dinner, Carolyn did it too! When Jenny wanted to go to aerobics at 6:00 a.m., Carolyn went with her. They visited each other's homes on weekends. And Jenny accompanied Carolyn not only to Bible study but also to large group meetings and conferences. Carolyn shared her time with Jenny—and her life too. Sometime during that fall, Jenny decided she wanted to follow Jesus and became a committed member of Carolyn's Bible study.

Now Jenny is a junior leading a Bible study in a residence hall at UCLA. She is investing her life in relationships with new students. She continues to grow closer to Jesus and to bring others with her.

There is more to leading a small group Bible study than planning for that weekly time slot. In fact, the small group meeting could be thought of as a rallying point for all that goes on during the week! In committing to be small group leaders, we have pledged to invest our time and our very lives in a group of people. Our goal is to intentionally influence them toward a closer relationship with Jesus and a life of following him.

Models from Scripture

The Bible is filled with examples of influencing relationships. Hannah and Eli apprenticed Samuel. Ruth dedicated herself to Naomi. David and Jonathan remained committed friends through incredible circumstances. Elijah passed the reins to Elisha. Elizabeth cared for her pregnant cousin, Mary. Jesus, being the model of investing in others for the sake of the kingdom, poured three years of his life into a diverse band of followers, giving special attention to three loud-mouthed fishermen (Peter, John and James), an "emotional female" (Mary of Bethany) and her over-responsible sister (Martha).

One of the most famous influencing relationships is the apostle Paul's with his young partner-in-ministry Timothy. Paul's farewell letter to his friend (2 Timothy) reveals the characteristics of their relationship that God used to help Timothy grow:

First, Paul relates closely to Timothy. He thanks God for him (1:3). Paul remembers Timothy in his prayers night and day (1:3). He longs to see him so he may be filled with joy (1:5). He knows Timothy's family and his history with Jesus well. It's obvious that Paul loves Timothy because he wants so much for him.

We dare not think of our small group members as projects to work on or our influencing as a program to put them through. God's mode of operation through history has been to influence people through close relationships, not ministry projects. Ask yourself, "Who am I close to, as Paul was to Timothy?"

Several years ago, I made a decision that hurt the feelings of a student I was discipling. She wrote me a card, expressing her hurt and anger. A colleague told me later how he watched my face fall and saw how distracted I became at a meeting after I read the card. I could not rest until I had reconciled with my friend. Her feelings mattered to me—because she mattered to me. It was the kind of relationship through which God could (and did) work.

A second key to Paul's influence is that he challenges Timothy. I see several direct hits on Timothy's weak spots in 2 Timothy 1—2. Paul challenges him to rekindle the gift God has given him (1:6). He calls him not to be ashamed of Paul and not to shrink from suffering for the gospel (1:8). Paul exhorts Timothy to keep the pattern of sound teaching he's heard from Paul—to guard the gospel entrusted to him (1:13-14). He challenges Timothy to be strong in Christ's grace, passing on the teaching he's learned to people who will "teach others also" (2:1-2). Paul reminds him to endure hardship (2:3), to reflect on these challenges (2:7) and to remember Jesus' example in all of it (2:8).

Some Christians have a bad attitude about challenging others to growth and obedience. This nursery rhyme, rather than the words of Scripture, may be their guide:

Little Bo Peep has lost her sheep

And can't tell where to find them.

Leave them alone, and they'll come home,

Wagging their tails behind them.

Yeah, right. We've all heard enough sermons about how dumb sheep are, and how we're just like them (and so, we need shepherds) to believe that! But when it comes to going after a "sheep" that's wandering away, scaling a cliff to retrieve one, carrying one back firmly and decisively, or actually using that hooked staff, we shy away.

Some of the harshest words I've read in the Bible are God's words to the "shepherds of Israel" in Ezekiel 34. They are not doing what it takes to care for God's flock, they are only thinking of themselves, and the sheep are scattering and getting eaten by wild animals.

When I consider those who have influenced me, I remember, in particular, Stan, an older student who cornered me at an InterVarsity camp one night after my sophomore year and really let me have it. Stan and I had been in a small group and then on a leadership team together all year. He always spent extra time talking to me, visiting me in my sorority and bringing me books and articles he thought would help me grow. He also was about the only one in our fellowship that wasn't fooled by my "together" appearance, discerning that I was actually living quite a double life, having a less-than-committed-to-Christ boyfriend and one time missing a leadership meeting because I had a hangover. Stan lovingly, but firmly, pointed out those issues in my life which were keeping me from following Jesus wholeheartedly. He would not let me wander away. I haven't been the same since that night fifteen years ago. How I appreciated someone loving me enough to risk challenging me! Stan was a good shepherd.

One final note on challenging others to grow: this kind of influence is *intentional.* We all have an amazing effect on people around us, whether we're planning to or not—sometimes for good, other times, not. The people in the relationships I'm describing weren't willing to leave it at that. When we're truly seeking to invest in someone, to challenge them to growth, we must be thinking about how to best do that, how to serve them, to encourage them and to help them grow. I am not advocating a six-weeks-fill-in-the-blanks-and-voilà!-you're-discipled-rigid-inflexible-insensitive plan. I am advocating the place for thoughtful and prayerful planning—for another's growth. To be intentional in challenging another to grow is to be a good steward of the relationships God has given us.

Finally, Paul models for Timothy. Paul understands the suffering he's calling Timothy to because he has endured it himself. He is writing to Timothy from a Roman prison, facing death by beheading. He knows how it feels to be rejected (1:15). He shares his honest trust that God will help him guard the gospel (1:12). Paul has not shrunk from the very calling he's shared with Timothy.

Just look at the life and ministry of Jesus to see how this works. All the healings his disciples witnessed, all the sermons they heard, all the tender conversations they overheard taught them by *showing* them how to love others. They watched while Jesus showed them how to do it—and next thing they knew, he was asking them to do it too! How many lessons came from incidents on their way somewhere or in conversations late at night or early in the morning? Because the disciples were always with Jesus, he could model everything for them. Because the disciples got to see what it looked like, they knew what to do.

The wonderful relationship between Jenny and Carolyn shows the power of modeling. As Carolyn simply was herself—and brought Jenny along—Jenny had the chance to see a real, live Christian, with ups and downs, live out her faith daily and in a variety of circumstances. When Carolyn spent time writing Jenny notes, when Carolyn jumped in to clean up the mess of a drunk—and vomiting—hallmate, and when Jenny and Carolyn spent the evening vacuuming the rooms of their neighbors "just because," Carolyn showed Jenny that being a Christian is serving, loving and extending yourself for people. I'm sure Carolyn was even a bad example at times—but Jesus used that, too, to show Jenny the nitty-gritties of following Jesus, repenting, making choices and being changed by him. Speaking about Carolyn, Jenny says, "Her life was the gospel." Jenny says that when she had her chance to clean up the mess of a drunk—and vomiting—hallmate last spring, she thought of Carolyn and got a sponge.

Living Out the Call to Influence Others

Most small group leaders will find that they are strong in one or two of the three elements of influence I've described and weak in the others. They might be strong on relationship and modeling, but weak on challenging (a love-blob). They might be strong on modeling and challenging, but weak on relationship (a drill-sergeant). They might be strong on relationship and challenge, but weak on modeling (two-faced). But something big is missing when anything is missing. We must be encouraged from the Scriptures and by our partners-in-ministry (staff, co-leaders, peers) to take risks in our weak areas.

Rhonda, a small group leader at UNLV, had a problem. She had been spending time with Mandy, a new student and member of her small group. They had become good friends in a short time, and Rhonda was excited to see Mandy growing in her faith. Then Mandy told Rhonda she was beginning a dating relationship with a nonbeliever. Rhonda herself had been way down that road before. She knew she needed to talk to Mandy about it, but Rhonda was afraid to confront Mandy.

Determined to be a faithful shepherd, Rhonda asked for prayer and accountability from the other small group leaders. During the time she'd set up to meet with Mandy, several of us met to pray for their conversation. Rhonda reported back that their talk went great. Mandy was really glad she brought up the relationship and wanted to do the right thing. Rhonda, like so many of us, knew she needed help to be a good influencer—and she got it!

No leader can be expected to have close relationships of challenging and modeling with every person in the group. All three elements can—and should—and will happen to some extent even in the weekly small group time. Your role as a small group leader is to make sure that everyone in your group is developing relationships with people who can help them grow—not to do it all yourself! Turn to co-leaders, older members of the group or staff. Encourage small group members to encourage each other

What small group leaders fear most

through times outside of the study. They can spend time praying for each other, reading books together, listening to each other or just having fun. The one-on-ones you set up each week can turn into powerful tools of God for mutual growth and encouragement.

Who should *you* invest in? Paul has good advice: "faithful people who will be able to teach others as well" (2 Timothy 2:2). Your first consideration should be for the continuation of your small group or the small group ministry in your particular area of campus. Choose people to invest in who could become fellow leaders and real partners with you. Ask, "Who is demonstrating not only a desire to learn from Jesus, but a desire to respond to his Word?" Who would jump at the chance to spend extra time with you, either one-on-one or with two or three others from the small group, for learning and growth? Who would you enjoy spending more time with? Who is working on some things that God has helped you with? Who has the potential to "teach others also," to join you in investing intentionally in the growth of others and building the kingdom on campus? Who would grow from the challenge to become a small group leader? Who would be someone you could see God using to bring others to himself? Those who are faithful to Jesus, those who are potential influencers (if not already!), those are the people to look for and to give your primary attention. Ask a staff member or older leader for help discerning who to focus on. Small group members who are especially enthusiastic right away might not turn out to be the most faithful. Those who warm up slowly may be hidden treasures.

Now, you'll only know the answers to the above questions by spending time with the people in your Bible study and talking it all over with Jesus and older partners-in-ministry. We've made it a goal in every fellowship I've worked with for small group leaders to spend one-one-one time with every member of their group during the first two weeks of school. This helps the members feel more connected during that critical start-up stage. It also helps leaders get a feel for who God has entrusted to them—and how not only to plan their group accordingly, but to consider who to spend more time with outside of the group meeting.

Putting It into Action

When you think you know who you'd like to spend more intentional time with, it's time to do a little dreaming about how you'd like to see your friend grow. The place to start is right where they are. As you talk with them and watch them, what do you think their growing edges are? What do they need to work on to be more like Jesus and follow him more closely? Are they spending regular time in prayer and personal Bible study? Are they growing as evangelists, learning how to share Jesus with those around them in a way that fits their personality? How about lifestyle issues? Are they struggling with sexual purity or substance abuse? How are they doing connecting their faith to their choice of major and use of time? How are they doing in relationships with others—does friendship come naturally or is trusting others difficult? How well do they know Jesus and the "basics" of Christian beliefs and disciplines? Consider their religious background; what might be missing in their lives? Your answers to those kinds of questions will help you get ideas for how to spend time with your friend and what would really help them grow.

When you get together, you'll want to describe some of the

Here are some general suggestions to give you a feel for what an influencing relationship might look like:

To build relationships

☐ Go to breakfast, lunch or dinner together.
☐ Tell each other about your day.
☐ Pray for each other together.
☐ Go to movies together.
☐ Go to each other's houses.
☐ Go grocery shopping together.
☐ Study together.
☐ Take a road trip.
☐ Write encouraging notes.
☐ Go to each other's "things" (performances, parties, presentations).
☐ Share your stuff.
☐ Listen.
☐ Be yourself.

To provide challenge

☐ Read a book together.
☐ Study the Bible together.
☐ Apply the Scriptures together.
☐ Discover and use your spiritual gifts.
☐ Co-lead Bible study.
☐ Show them how to invest in younger Christians.
☐ Engage in outreach together.

(continued on next page)

ideas you've come up with. Together you can decide what you'd like to do, especially if it involves some kind of study or reading (you can be more casual—in approach, not in intention—about the relationship-building stuff). Usually, younger students or newer Christians benefit from studies and help with things like lifestyle issues, Bible study and prayer, and understanding Jesus and Christianity better. With older students or more mature ones, you can work on quite a variety of things, like how to use money, the theology of prayer, conflict resolution skills, self-esteem issues, vocational stewardship or what it means for them to be an adult child of an alcoholic. It appears that part of being a good friend is being up for anything that would be helpful!

Well Worth the Effort

It will cost us to be small group leaders who take seriously the call to intentionally influence others. Relationships take time. Challenging takes emotional energy and thought. Modeling requires willingness to lay out our lives for others to see. We might be rejected or misunderstood. We might be disappointed with the results of our investment of time and energy. It might hurt—our grades, our personal plans or

(continued from last page)
☐ Pray for each other.
☐ Confront as necessary.
☐ Encourage a lot.
☐ Affirm whenever you get the chance.
☐ Make use of resources within your fellowship like large group meetings, discipleship conferences, camps, ministry experiences, staff and older students.
☐ Make use of resources outside your fellowship like pastors, church ministries, Christian counselors and therapists, recovery groups.

To be a good model

☐ Make it a point to share personal struggles, concerns and ask for prayer.
☐ Read and apply chapter eleven, "Growing as a Leader."
☐ Be in relationships of accountability and challenge for your growth.
☐ Model hospitality and generosity with your home, possessions and time.
☐ Take risks in outreach and bring members with you.
☐ Know that the best way to be like Jesus in your relationships is to be close to him—and keep developing your own responsiveness to him.

our feelings—to commit ourselves to another's growth.

When I make a mental list of those I consider treasured friends, the joys of my life, I realize that most of them began as members of my small group or a team I worked with. They were the people I believed God wanted me to invest in more deeply. And as we spent all those hours together, they became not only my friends, but influencers too. What a joy to see people not only grow closer to Jesus but also to bring others to him! What a thrill to be part of the lives of those who are deepening their relationship with God and ministering to others. It helps me grow too.

Understanding the Chapter
Study

1. Read Acts 9:1-31. We usually think of this as a passage about conversion. But look at the people God uses in Saul's life. Who are they?

2. What risks do they take?

3. What is the outcome of their faithfulness in caring for Saul?

Reflect

1. Do some journaling beginning with these questions: Who has helped you know Jesus better and be more like him? How did the person do it? What did you learn? What can you imitate in that person's example as an influencer?

2. Of the three components of influence—relationship, challenge and modeling—which is your strength? your weakness?

How do you know?

3. What ideas will help you grow in your areas of weakness?

Apply

1. Who are the "faithful people" in your current small group?
Why do you think so?

2. Who from your group can you begin spending time with?
What do you think his or her "growing edges" are?

3. Who in your life currently is influencing you and helping you grow?

4. Who can you ask to spend time with you as you lead a small group? Depending on how your fellowship is organized, it will probably be your small group coordinator or area coordinator. It could also be a staff-worker, pastor, older Christian in your fellowship or church, or simply a strong peer relationship. Make plans to ask someone or to take full advantage of the organizational structures set up for just that purpose.

13/THE ORGANIZING LEADER
■ Ann Beyerlein

A follow-up card with the name of a student who has indicated interest in InterVarsity and possibly a small group is about to escape John's awareness. John has met many new people this year, some within twenty-four hours of receiving their names, but he is tired and his attitude is degenerating. Here is yet one more person who may only have signed the card for a free hot dog at the picnic. John sticks the card under the edge of his answering machine, thinking he'll visit the person tomorrow. John figures another day or two won't make much difference. Sure, John will pray for the student, but, after all, they are adults,, and if they are really interested, they'll find out who the Bible study leader is in their dorm. John hopes his dorm group will come together in a spontaneous way. He's really not interested in going where no one has gone before.

Days pass. The card is faded from the sun and stained from the Coke

John spilled on it. One evening the phone rings and it's Susie, the Inter-Varsity small group coordinator, wondering how John's follow-up is going. She is particularly interested in whether or not he's met Dan Hernandez, as she met him at the picnic, and he was interested in a small group. John's mind races as he tries to think of who in the world Dan is. Suddenly, John spots the faded, stained card, and in his haste in grabbing it, overturns the answering machine onto the floor. Yes, he tells Susie, he's looking forward to meeting Dan and in fact he's going down to Dan's room right now to see if he's in. John springs into action, thinking it may not be a bad idea to get a little organized.

Often we see organization and management as unspiritual parts of Christian leadership. And this is true if the only goal is smooth Christian programming, without much flexibility or reliance on prayer and the Holy Spirit. However, if, like John, we stop planning our spiritual  tasks, we can become forgetful or careless, and our ministry may be hurt.

Jesus and Organization

Jesus knew that some simple organization was necessary to complete a task when he fed the five thousand. After Jesus realized that the disciples had found only five loaves and two fish to feed the crowd he was teaching,

> He ordered them [the disciples] to get all the people to sit down in groups on the green grass. So they sat down in groups of hundreds and of fifties. Taking the five loaves and the two fish, he looked up to heaven, and blessed and broke the loaves, and gave them to his disciples to set before the people; and he divided the two fish among them all. And all ate and were filled; and they took up twelve baskets full of broken pieces and of the fish. Those who had eaten the loaves numbered five thousand men. (Mark 6:39-44 NRSV)

Jesus directed the disciples to divide the crowd into smaller groups so this large group could be managed without chaos. Then he had the disciples distribute the bread and gather up the leftovers. With Jesus providing organization, a potential stampede was avoided, many people were served, and they probably had a great experience together.

As small group leaders, we can be faithful in contacting and caring for the people Jesus has given to us like the disciples were in Mark 6. The disciples weren't doing glamorous work. And sometimes our work involves the unappealing tasks of phone calls, cleaning our rooms or apartments and visiting strangers like Dan, in order that as many people as possible can be fed by the Word of God.

Hitting the Ground Running

The stability of the campus ministry for a particular school year often lies in what happens in the first two weeks. It is critical that we are visible so that those interested can find us early on, and it is vital that we contact these people and get them involved in fellowship as soon as possible. The more names received during new student outreach, the more chance a chapter has for successful small groups. For example, at a commuter school if there aren't enough names received from one neighborhood, there won't be a small group in that area and interested people may fall through the cracks. If students get established in a fellowship while they are still interested and have openings in their schedules, there is a much greater chance of their staying involved.

It's not too late for John. He has talked to his chapter leaders, and he knows the type of group he will lead. Bolting down the hall to meet Dan, John has adjusted his attitude and is glad he's getting back on track. But, wait. What is John going to say when he arrives?

Often whether or not a person attends a small group even once lies in the initial encounters with the small group leader. This is especially key if the leader and potential member have never met. John remembers this and suddenly stops in his tracks, collects his thoughts and reminds himself of what he learned in small group leader's training during the role-play with potential members. John says a quick prayer. With confidence, he

sticks the card in his pocket and knocks on the door. Below are some of the things John says:

"Hi, I'm John. Are you Dan?"

"I got your name from InterVarsity. I live in this dorm, and they said you might like some information about our group. Do you have a minute?"

"How's it going for you so far on campus?" "Do you have any questions about InterVarsity?"

"So, have you been involved with Christian fellowship before? What was it like?"

"InterVarsity is having a meeting tomorrow night and some of us in the dorm are going. Would you like to come?"

"Oh, by the way, I'm the InterVarsity small group leader in our dorm. Do you have a minute for me to tell you about my small group?"

"A group of six or eight of us from this dorm will get together each week, and I'll lead a discussion on one passage of Scripture. It's neat because you get everybody's ideas, and you don't have to know anything about the Bible to come. It's not Bible trivia."

"Our group is a lot more than a Bible discussion. We pray for each other and have fun together. Last year the people in my small group even went camping together once. A number of the people in the group became my best friends on campus. When I was struggling through chemistry, they were the people who were there for me. We also invited some people from our dorm who had never studied the Bible before, and they didn't hate it! The first meeting will last about an hour. Would you like me to let you know more details?"

"Is there any particular night you know you absolutely can't come?"

Wow! John had some great questions. He immediately told Dan who he was and why he was there. Depending on Dan's responses, the questions above may have changed or have occurred during later conversations. Sometimes in the first visit with a stranger, it is best to just get to know them and maybe invite them to some kind of general activity.

Telling someone about the small group too soon or saying too much may be overwhelming for them. Waiting a couple of days until you know the person a little better might make them more likely to really consider it. When it's time to invite the student to small group, don't assume the person knows what it is; explain it appropriately. Remember that often people won't come to something they don't understand. If John had known Dan and had some idea of his spiritual maturity, he could have made his explanation more detailed about the type of group that he would be leading and given more of his vision for the small group.

If at all possible, it's best to make follow-up contacts in person. More trust can be built, and you can notice body language. For example, Kimiko may be saying yes, but everything in her body language is saying no. Seeing her body language will help you to be sensitive to her needs and not too pushy. Often people will say what you want to hear just to get you off the phone and not follow through, or they will say no quickly because they don't feel like they know you. However, if you do have to use the phone, the

Inviting People to Small Group: A Role-Play for Training Small Group Leaders

Here's a great preparation exercise to do with other small group leaders.

Half of the leaders should play the role of small group leader, using some of John's questions earlier in the chapter. The other half can play potential small group members who have taken on one of the following characters. These students have all signed cards or somehow indicated interest in InterVarsity. The leaders will have to adjust their questions and comments depending on the responses they receive. The leaders may have met the person briefly before, but there was no chance to talk about InterVarsity or spiritual things.

Debrief the role-play by talking about what you learned, what the leaders did well and what other ideas you have about

(continued on next page)

same kinds of questions will work.

Things to Do Before the First Small Group Meeting

John is on his way, but has some work to do before his first meeting. Here's his checklist.

☐ *Pray.* John was faithful in praying for his small group all summer, but since he's been back on campus, his prayer has dropped off. John immediately begins praying about his follow-up appointments, possible group members and his first meeting.

☐ *Publicize small group.* Posters around the dorm or in the music school might solicit some interest for small group. If the group is not based in a particular dorm, announcements at large group may be appropriate. John retrieves the small group posters that Susie gave him from under his bed and puts them up. O.k., so organization isn't John's gift, but he's doing it!

☐ *Receive names and form a potential list.* Often small group leaders receive names from the small group coordinator or can ask chapter leaders for possible names of people who might be interested in the type of small group they want to lead. Often just thinking through some of our own acquaintances can yield some interesting people who might want to come. John shouldn't miss those obvious students who are Christians but maybe

(continued from last page) approaching strangers.

Character One: John/Joyce has grown up in the church and definitely wants to be involved in a Christian fellowship on campus but is not sure which one. He/she wants to study the Bible but in the past has studied the Bible only in large group lecture settings like a youth group devotional.

Character Two: John/Joyce became a Christian last summer through some high-school friends. There is no doubt that this is a genuine conversion. He/she has been to church a couple of times but has no real concept of Christian fellowship.

Character Three: John/Joyce signed a card for InterVarsity because a roommate invited him/her to an InterVarsity picnic, not because he/she is a Christian. He/she enjoyed the people at the picnic and is open to investigating spiritual things while at college.

haven't come to his fellowship.

☐ *Obtain Bible discussion materials.* Many chapters provide Bible studies for the first weeks or quarter. A staffworker or student leader can also provide suggestions.

☐ *Follow up on those names.* John has a great start on his follow-up. He knows what to say, and he has met one person. John needs to speak personally to everyone on his list at least once before the first meeting.

☐ *Discuss the small group.* John needs to explain the small group to each person on the list and discuss potential times for the small group to have an organizational meeting.

☐ *Set organizational meeting date* for the first or second week of classes. This may mean calling everyone one more time. Keep going, John!

☐ *Remind everyone of the meeting the day of the meeting.* Offer to eat dinner with or pick up any potentially hesitant members.

☐ *Make physical preparations.* Buy food, clean your room, check with your roommate, turn down the telephone ringer and whatever you do, John, don't forget this meeting or be late.

Commuter schools, smaller or newer chapters might choose to organize their small groups differently in the preliminary stages. For example, early in the school year the large group meeting might be a good place to break into small groups after, or in place of, a speaker. This helps everyone become familiar with the small group experience. On some campuses chapter leaders may be finding small group leaders at the same time they are finding small group members. As students bond and learn the concept,

Used by permission of Rob Suggs.

hey may be able to move their group to another time and place. A chapter might also decide to begin with one large small-group with a well-trained leader and excellent activities that will ensure a positive experience for students as a foundation for future groups. Thematic or single-sex small groups or groups that appeal to felt needs of students like support groups might also be a good way to organize small groups and catch the interest of new people.

John is psyched. It's the day of his meeting, and he has an hour to prepare. He's bought m & m's and has a great icebreaker question that will get everyone talking. He knows he wants to do a short Bible discussion on Acts 2:40-47, so he reads the passage a number of times and then chooses a number of good discussion questions, some from the guide (see sidebar on p. 198) and a couple he wrote himself.

After completing the Bible discussion preparation, John is vaguely aware of the need to do a couple of other things at his first meeting. John gets up and digs through his wastepaper basket, looking for the sheet Susie gave him on the first small group meeting. Here's what John finds.

Things to Do at the First Small Group Meeting

1. Be ready ahead of time. Make sure the room is comfortable, and arrange chairs and couches so that everyone can be seen and see one another. If you don't have enough chairs, it's better to have everyone on the floor. That way people aren't on different levels. Find yourself a seat where you can make eye contact with everyone. Have refreshments ready and some extra Bibles on hand.

2. Begin with an icebreaker. (John remembered this part.) Tell people to take as many m & m's as they need. If someone has the most red m & m's, they talk about a favorite movie. Green: a proud moment. Yellow: a family member, and so on. Watch that this doesn't take too long.

3. Talk about the group briefly, clearly and with enthusiasm. Show them you have some goals.

☐ Tell the group what will happen at this first meeting and how long it will last in order to put them at ease.

☐ Explain the type of group this is.

☐ Talk about some ideas for prayer, building community and Bible discussion. Really emphasize community!

☐ Mention that you hope to find a group of people who will be committed to the group and thus will benefit more from it. You might ask those who attend for a four-week commitment to the group which will be followed by an evaluation.

☐ Encourage them to bring friends to the group at any time.

☐ Talk about the mission field for the group.

4. Go over some of the ground rules for Bible discussion. (See pages 66-67.) Telling the group the type of Bible study this is puts people at ease and will alleviate problems of people talking too much and bringing in a lot of extraneous information. You may need to repeat goals and ground rules at the first few meetings, especially for new people. At the first meeting you could say something like: "We are going to be discussing one passage from the New Testament. I am the discussion leader, not the teacher, and we will learn together. To keep us on the same level, let's just look at the passage under discussion. It would be great if everyone would talk."

An Introductory Bible Discussion: The First Christian Fellowship—Acts 2:40-47

Introduction: Acts 2:1-12 tells what happened on the day of Pentecost when the believers were all filled with the Holy Spirit and spoke of the mighty works of God in a variety of languages. Acts 2:14-40 is Peter's evangelistic sermon to the cosmopolitan crowd in Jerusalem. He challenges them to believe in Jesus, repent and save themselves from the "corrupt generation."

In the passage we are studying today, Acts 2:40-47, we will see what characterizes the *new generation* of believers. From this example, we will discover what should happen in our life together as a small group.

Approach question: Talk about the best small group of two to fifteen people you've been in. This doesn't have to be a religious group or your family. It could be a sports team or a club. Tell why it was the best.

Study questions: 1. Read Acts 2:40-47. Looking at the whole passage, what words would you pick to describe this Christian fellowship of 3,000?

2. How might the group life in the early church have been in sharp contrast to the "corrupt generation" from which they were being saved?

3. The new believers were baptized and then very devoted. What does it mean to be devoted to something?

4. How do you picture the fellowship described in verse 42?

5. How can or might we increase
(continued on next page)

5. Begin the Bible discussion with prayer and background information. This puts the passage in context.

6. Ask the Bible discussion questions you have prepared. Be ready to drop some if you run out of time. Don't worry if there is some silence at the meeting, and don't answer all of your own questions. If a question has already been answered, drop it. Contribute to the application time. The group will be only as vulnerable as the leader.

7. Close in prayer. The closing prayer will depend on the group and the time factor. The leader may need to offer a prayer for the whole group.

8. Make announcements. Decide together the time and place of the next meeting and mention other chapter activities.

John reads through the sheet and thinks about how to put his vision for the group in his own words. It's now 6:45 p.m. John makes his bed. He's excited and nervous about how everything will go.

There is a knock on the

door. Someone's early. Dan Hernandez walks through the door, Bible in hand, and John knows that his small group is really off the ground.

Ongoing Organization

John had a great first meeting. He is so glad he got himself organized. About half of the people he invited attended the first small group, which is even better than normal. But the need to organize hasn't passed. Because Kathy has come once doesn't mean that she will come, or even remember to come again.

John decides to try to have some personal contact with each person in his small group before the second meeting. (This is where a co-leader comes in handy.) He plays basketball with Dan, invites Kendra and her roommate to church, and spends some time with people on the phone. Susie suggests John reinvite people on his list to the second small group—especially those who seemed interested or said they would come and then didn't.

(continued from last page)
our commitment to the things mentioned in verse 42?

Leader's note: These early Christians were devoted to the apostles' teaching or Bible study, the fellowship (each other), the breaking of bread—the Lord's Supper (the breaking of bread in verse 46 probably refers to eating together)—and prayer. Some people in your small group this first night might not want to increase their commitment to these things, so don't overwhelm them. Maybe have a couple people share briefly.

Another option: What is one healthy thing that you want to be committed or devoted to this semester or quarter, no matter what happens?

6. Note the last sentence: "And the Lord added to their number daily those who were being saved." What could unbelievers have observed in the Christian community which would draw them to salvation (verses 43-47)?

7. How might the way the believers regarded their possessions have been a sign to outsiders?

8. What changes in lifestyle do we need to make to be a clearer sign to outsiders that Christ has made a difference in our lives?

9. How might a small group in a dorm or fraternity (or off-campus) reflect some of these things?

Summary: Talk about how your group can be devoted to the Scriptures, fellowship and community, worship and prayer, and the resulting outreach.

At John's second meeting he has half the people from the first night and the rest are new. John prays daily that God will solidify his group. John's goal is to have a group of committed attenders in place by the fourth meeting. Susie suggests that although John has mentioned it in small group, he also talk individually to some more interested students about coming on a weekly basis and possibly helping in group leadership and management.

After talking with John, Kendra says she is willing to spend time with some of the women on John's list, and Dan says he's willing to bring refreshments. But what does John do about people who seemed interested or said that they would come but still haven't made it? Susie says that if the people seemed to have genuine interest, John should go back one more time; he might even ask the students if they want John to keep inviting them. During these early weeks, John also spends some time helping people who couldn't come the night of his small group find another group on campus.

John's stopping by Kathy's room and talking about her personal life as well as her questions about Christianity becomes instrumental in her becoming a Christian. Kathy had a lot of questions during the Acts 2 Bible study. She especially wondered what Luke meant when he said that "the Lord added to their number daily those who were being saved." She has no concept of salvation and a minimal church background. One night, John has the privilege of praying with Kathy as she becomes a Christian.

Doug is someone who always seems happy when John stops by his room. They have had some good conversations, a number of them about the Christian faith and Doug's home church. Doug hasn't made it to small group but wants John to reinvite him. After about a month, Doug says he just doesn't have time for the small group in his schedule. Because of the trust in their relationship, John decides to challenge Doug and ask him what could be more important than small group. Doug finally begins to take his spiritual life seriously and attends a small group meeting. From then on, Doug never misses a meeting, and today credits John's loving persistence for some of his spiritual growth and subsequent full-time Christian work.

Sally came to the first small group meeting and was quiet for the entire meeting. Now she regularly avoids John, and it's obvious she doesn't want another invitation. John feels awkward and sad about his lack of relationship with Sally. Susie tells John that unfortunately this is not uncommon, and there could be a million reasons for Sally's self-consciousness. Some small groups never even develop because there aren't enough interested people. However, Susie assures John that God is pleased with his faithfulness in inviting Sally and others like her.

By week five, John's small group is moving toward warp speed, beginning to lead itself. The regular attenders do an evaluation and set some new goals for the group. The students are becoming more comfortable with each other, and John can concentrate on using his gifts of pastoring and discussion-leading. Every Sunday afternoon John spends some time thinking about his small group. He jots down who he needs to call, plans part of the meeting, thinks about future needs and prays for his group. John is on a roll; he's an organization machine.

Just before Christmas, Susie asks John what he'll do to organize his group for second semester. John realizes he'll have to set a new course as his group will need to meet on a different day and time. He also commits himself to reinvite some people from his first semester list and invite some new people who have come to mind. With Susie, John also sets one goal for each small group component for his group second semester. Below is John's list.

Community: Take one small group time early in the semester to discuss each member's spiritual lifeline.

Nurture: Ask more application questions during the Bible discussion and encourage answers. Follow up the next week on how people applied the Scripture.

Worship and Prayer: Work more on conversational prayer, helping the group pray short prayers as they listen to each other.

Outreach: Invite 2+, not-yet-Christian friends to play volleyball with the small group some Saturday.

John never realized that leading a small group would be this much work. However, John is glad he explored this strange new world. Because he spent some time organizing his list and systematically calling and reinviting people to the group, he now has five new friends, has seen someone become a Christian and has the chance to see the Word of God feeding students who once were only names on now beloved follow-up cards.

This is the work of a small group leader. At times the journey will be rocky, but with this book in hand you are well-equipped. Are you ready to accept your mission?

Understanding the Chapter
Study

1. In Acts 16 Paul organizes a very diverse small group that will eventually become the church at Philippi. Read Acts 16:6-40. What type of people end up in this small group?

2. How does Paul demonstrate obedience, perseverance and follow-up?

3. How might verses 12 and 13 illustrate some planning and strategy?

4. Why is verse 40 important?

After Paul left, Luke may have stayed to help this group develop.

Reflect

1. How did you get involved in your first small group?

2. Think about your gifts as an organizer. What will help you complete the tasks necessary to get your small group off the ground?

3. Think about your feelings toward follow-up. What will help you get over any fears of taking initiative?

Apply

Spend some time thinking about your small group before it begins. Depending on your chapter situation, you can consider the type of group you will lead, gather materials, list names of potential people for your group and list favorite icebreakers. If you know the people in your group, you can set more definite goals for the four components.

Spend some time praying for yourself. Ask God to help you be a faithful people-gatherer for your small group. Ask him to give you courage and obedience. Pray for your group and whatever you know about your situation. God knows the rest.